English for you

by Jackie Head and Roy Blatchford

Hutchinson
London   Melbourne   Auckland   Johannesburg

Hutchinson Education
An imprint of Century Hutchinson Ltd
62–65 Chandos Place, London WC2N 4NW

Century Hutchinson Australia Pty Ltd
P O Box 496, 16–22 Church Street, Hawthorn,
Melbourne, Victoria 3122, Australia

Century Hutchinson New Zealand Limited
P O Box 40–086, Glenfield, Auckland 10,
New Zealand

Century Hutchinson South Africa (Pty) Ltd
P O Box 337, Bergvlei 2012, South Africa

First published 1988

Designed by Keely and McMahon, Bristol

Set in 11 on 12½pt Century Schoolbook and 11 on 12½
Univers Light by D P Press

Printed and bound in Great Britain

British Library Cataloguing in Publication Data
Head, Jackie
    English for you.
    1. English language—Grammar—1950-
    I. Title   II. Blatchford, Roy
    428   PE1112

    ISBN 0–09–172959–9

Artwork by Juliet Breese

The Publishers would like to thank the following for
permission to use their photographs:

Ardea Photographics page 107; Associated Press Ltd page
88; BBC Hulton Picture Library page 82 (bottom), 89 and
90; Camera Press page 53, 82 and 126; Camerapix page
116; Farmers Weekly page 55; Melanie Friend page 49;
Geoffe Goode Photographer page 65; Sally and Richard
Greenhill page 10, 21, 24, 94, 97 and 119; *The Guardian*
page 48; Imperial War Museum page 46 and 51; Mary
Evans Picture Library page 113; Novosti Press Agency
page 47; WHO/UN page 17.

English for you
Contents

Skills Section

Jackie Head is an English teacher and runs a Learning Support Department at William Ellis School, London.

Roy Blatchford is Head Teacher of Bicester Community College, Oxfordshire.

How to use this book

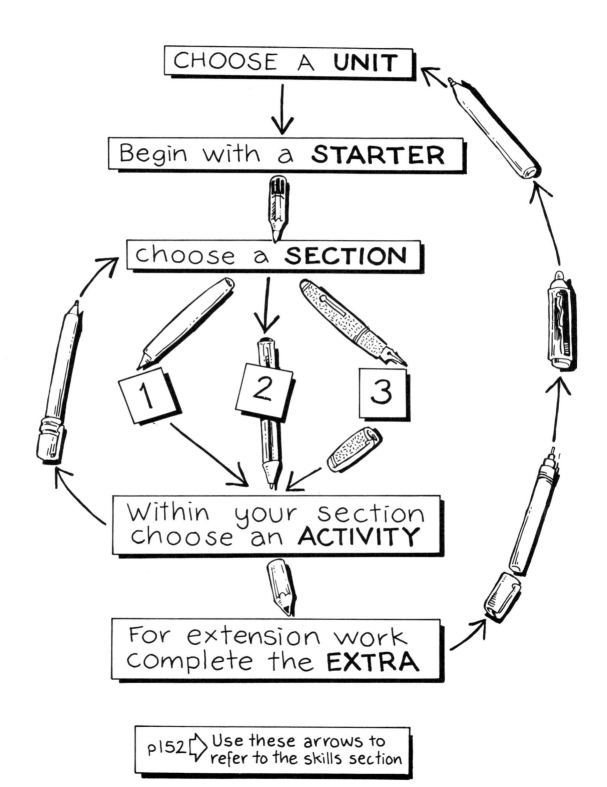

CHOOSE A **UNIT**

Begin with a **STARTER**

choose a **SECTION**

1   2   3

Within your section choose an **ACTIVITY**

For extension work complete the **EXTRA**

p152 ➪ Use these arrows to refer to the skills section

Bonds

starter Gangs

Bonds are the close ties of friendship and trust, which link people together. Often they are formed through the family, or through love, and sometimes through the feeling of loyalty to close friends.

West Side Story is a musical set in New York. Two rival gangs, the 'Jets' and the 'Sharks' are fighting over the neighbourhood 'turf'. The story is loosely based on Shakespeare's *Romeo and Juliet*, in that it tells of two people who fall in love, despite the fact that their families are at war. This extract is from a song sung by the Jets at the beginning of the musical.

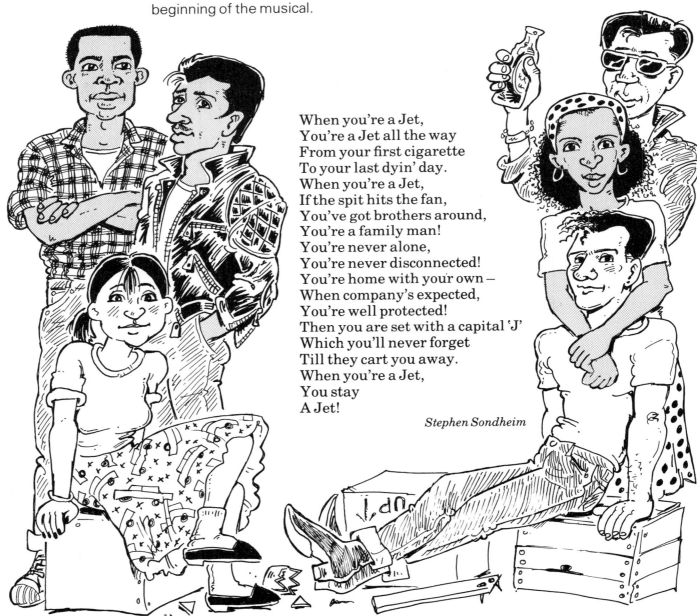

When you're a Jet,
You're a Jet all the way
From your first cigarette
To your last dyin' day.
When you're a Jet,
If the spit hits the fan,
You've got brothers around,
You're a family man!
You're never alone,
You're never disconnected!
You're home with your own –
When company's expected,
You're well protected!
Then you are set with a capital 'J'
Which you'll never forget
Till they cart you away.
When you're a Jet,
You stay
A Jet!

Stephen Sondheim

The following poem shows a boy who has cut himself off from friendship.

One of the Boys

My name . . . Well, that don't matter,
But I goes to this 'ere school,
And I've got a reputation
For breaking every rule.
The teachers, they all hates me,
Every master I annoys,
'Cos I'm a right old criminal –
Dead smart, one of the boys.

The first day at me new school
Me teacher got right shocked,
'Cos straight away I lost me cap –
That's how the lav got blocked!
And I burns me new blazer
Hiding gaspers in me pocket,
And I decides, in this 'ere boat,
It's me is gonna rock it.

Next day the form's dead eager
As through the gates they swarm,
And they elects some swatty clot
As captain of the form.
Now so far I've gone easy,
Just sizing up the dump,
But when I sees what that job's worth,
I gives that clot a clump.

So he resigns, and after
I've persuaded all the rest,
I gets elected. Then I starts
To feather my own nest.
I helps with dinner money –
Of course, I takes my cut –
The teacher couldn't work it out,
And he promptly done his nut.

So the teachers they all hates me,
Every master I annoys,
'Cos I'm a right old criminal –
Dead smart, one of the boys.

You lot goes to Assembly,
But me, I'm never there.
I sits, and has a crafty smoke
Down the – well you know where.
Then I copies some kid's homework,
And if I gets found out,
I makes him say he copied mine,
Or I punch him up the snout.

In Art, old Ginger goes out front –
He looks a right old case.
We're all supposed to paint him,

So I does – right on his face.
In History I writes to Jean,
Saying I loves her true.
I write the same to Madge in French,
And in Maths I writes to Lou.

Each week I goes down Soho,
Buys a tanner sexy book,
And charges all the prefects
Half a dollar for a look.
Then I leads 'em back o' the fives courts,
And I plays my cards dead cool,
'Cos while you lot do lessons,
I runs a different kind of school.

So as my innocent years roll by
I'm in on every racket,
And anyone who tries it on,
He quickly cops a packet.
Till in the fourth year I can claim
To be the school's real boss,
And I spends me time in dodging work,
'Cos work, that's a dead loss.

So the teachers, they all hates me,
Every master I annoys,
'Cos I'm a right old criminal –
Dead smart, one of the boys.

One day, when it was raining hard,
I pinched some small kids mac.
But he must have seen me do it,
'Cos the basket pinched it back.
Now I can't stand kids what pinches things –
Least, not from me, the get,
So I sound the flipping fire alarm,
And everyone get wet.

Our form gets up a football team.
Of course, I wasn't picked,
So when they left the field they found
Their money had been nicked.
But though they're all dead stupid,
They guessed I'd had a go,
So when I tries to talk to them,
They just don't want to know.

Then last week, down the billiard hall,
I joins up with a mob,
And we breaks into some radio shop –
A very crafty job,
Till some dirty copper spots us,
And I'm the one gets caught.
And there's no one who'll stand by me
Next week when I'm in court.

And you can't help feeling rotten,
When you stand about and wait
For some bloke who'll say 'Hello' to you
But there's no one thinks of me.
But I don't care. When I'm big time
I'll show you – wait and see,
All you teachers, you what hates me,
Every master I annoys,
'Cos I'm a right old criminal . . .
Dead smart . . . One of the boys . . .

William Samson

think

1 In what ways are the Jets loyal to one another? How might reactions and feelings differ if it were a group of girls?
2 Select the words and phrases in the poem which suggest that being in a group is preferable to being alone.
3 Imagine what it would be like to be a Jet yourself. Talk about what you would do and where you would go. Think about:
   ● your clothes;
   ● your tastes in music;
   ● the ways in which you might pass the time.
   How might the Sharks differ?
4 Are there any ways in which the boy in 'One of the Boys' has a life you would envy?

choose

a Write a piece of scripted conversation between *either* the Sharks and the Jets, *or* within one of the two gangs.
b Write a song which might have been written by a member of a particular group. Think carefully about the qualities needed to be part of that group, and the type of language they would use.
c Do you think gangs are a menace to society or a useful way for young people to make friends? Prepare a 300 word report on your views which can be used as the basis for an oral or written assignment. You should consider:
   ● having a sense of identity;
   ● self-protection;
   ● vandalism caused by gangs of youths;
   ● sharing interests and values with others of your age.
d Pick out the words and phrases which indicate when and where the poems were written. Rewrite one of the poems in a different setting in time and/or place.

1

Romance

Read through the following poems and then answer the questions which follow.

Rondeau Redoublé

There are so many kinds of awful men –
One can't avoid them all. She often said
She'd never make the same mistake again:
She always made a new mistake instead.

The chinless type who made her feel ill-bred;
The practised charmer, less than charming when
He talked about the wife and kids and fled –
There are so many kinds of awful men.

The half-crazed hippy, deeply into Zen,
Whose cryptic homilies she came to dread;
The fervent youth who worshipped Tony Benn –
'One can't avoid them all,' she often said.

The ageing banker, rich and overfed,
Who held forth on the dollar and the yen –
Though there were many more mistakes ahead,
She'd never make the same mistake again.

The budding poet, scribbling in his den
Odes not to her but to his pussy, Fred;
The drunk who fell asleep at nine or ten –
She always made a new mistake instead.

And so the gambler was at least unwed
And didn't preach or sneer or wield a pen
Or hoard his wealth or take the Scotch to bed.
She'd lived and learned and lived and learned but then
There are so many kinds.

Wendy Cope

I'm really very fond

I'm really very fond of you,
he said.

I don't like fond.
It sounds like something
you would tell a dog.

Give me love,
or nothing.

Throw your fond in a pond,
I said.

But what I felt for him
was also warm, frisky,
moist-mouthed,
eager,
and could swim away

if forced to do so.

Alice Walker

think   Use the following questions as the basis of a discussion.

1   Pick out the words and phrases which you like most in each poem, and give reasons for your choice.
2   Both poems use repetition, rhymes and a chosen rhythm. Pick out the uses of these in each poem.
3   The title 'Rondeau Redoublé' refers to the *form* of the poem. Look closely at the construction of the verses, and the repetition of words and phrases and try to work out what the rondeau redoublé form is.
4   In what ways are the attitudes of the two poems similar?
5   Would the poems differ if it were a man speaking?

choose   a   Write your own rondeau redoublé poem.
         b   Write a poem which relies on repetition.
         c   Write a report on your opinions of the two poems. You will need to discuss your views on:
              ● the form they use;
              ● the vocabulary chosen;
              ● the messages put across.

Below is a story about a romantic relationship. The paragraphs have been muddled up and need re-ordering.

First kiss

1 She looked at me and smiled, and said, 'You're nice.' And then she laid her head on my shoulders, it was nice and warm. I was just about to kiss her when she sort of moved her head a bit, and quickly I moved my head backwards and my heart started to beat.

5 Then I started thinking again: 'Should I kiss her?' I didn't know what to do, I wasn't even concentrating on the film. The next minute I knew, I had my arms around her.

2 I met her outside the cinema, but I was there first, a bit scared because it was my first time, and I was thinking, saying to myself 'Should I kiss her?' If I did it would be for the first time.

6 Then suddenly she jumped out; she nearly scared me to death. So we went in, bought something to eat, then we sat down. The film had already started. We didn't say a word; we just sat there as if we didn't know each other.

3 My first kiss happened when I went out with my first girl. I met her at a party and she was nice so I asked her out and she said 'Yes.' So I asked if she would like to go to the pictures and she agreed.

7 Then I said: 'Is this your first time?' She said: 'Yes.' And then carried on watching the film. Her name was Sandra.

Yip Wing Lu

4 Then this time my head slowly moved towards her head, our lips touched. It was like the nicest thing I have ever had, then I moved away. It was my first kiss.
Then the film ended and I walked home with my arms around her.

Place them in the order which you think is the most appropriate, using the paragraph numbers rather than writing out the whole story. Before you finally decide on the order, see if you can answer the following questions about the story.

think

1 Is there a sentence or phrase which sounds as though it is the beginning or ending of the story?
2 Are there events which depend on something else happening first?
3 Does the story flow naturally from one paragraph to another?
4 Does the sequence of time make sense?

Very often it seems that the two people involved in a romantic relationship, experience that single relationship very differently. On the next page are two extracts from *Look Back In Anger* by John Osborne which illustrate this point. Read the passages through carefully and then answer the questions which follow.

Jimmy and Alison are a married couple. Jimmy describes their wedding day.

Jimmy: The last time she was in church was when she was married to me. I expect that surprises you doesn't it? It was expediency, pure and simple, we were in a hurry you see. *(The comedy of this strikes him at once and he laughs.)* Yes, we were actually in a hurry! Lusting for the slaughter! Well, the local registrar was a particular pal of Daddy's, and we knew he'd spill the beans to the colonel like a shot. So we had to seek out some local vicar who didn't know him quite so well. But it was no use. When my best man – a chap I'd met in the pub that morning – and I turned up, Mummy and Daddy were in the church already. They'd found out at the last moment, and had come to watch the execution carried out. How I remember looking down at them, full of beer for breakfast and feeling a bit buzzed. Mummy was slumped over a pew in a heap – the noble, female rhino polaxed at last! And Daddy sat beside her, upright and unafraid, dreaming of his days among the Indian Princes, and unable to believe he'd left his horsewhip at home. Just the two of them in that empty church – them and me. *(Coming out of his remembrance suddenly.)* I'm not sure what happened after that. We must have been married, I suppose. I think I remember being sick in the vestry. *(To Alison.)* Was I?

Alison describes their first meeting to her friend Helena.

Helena: It's almost unbelievable. I don't understand your part in it at all. Why? That's what I don't see. Why did you –

Alison: Marry him? There must be about six different answers. When the family came back from India, everything seemed, I don't know – unsettled? Anyway, Daddy seemed remote and rather irritable. And Mummy – well, you know Mummy. I didn't have much to worry about. I didn't know I was born as Jimmy says. I met him at a party. I remember it so clearly. I was almost twenty-one. The men there looked as though they distrusted him, and the women, they were all intent on showing their contempt for this rather odd creature, but no one seemed quite sure how to do it. He'd come to the party on a bicycle, he told me, and there was oil all over his dinner jacket. It had been such a lovely day, and he'd been in the sun. Everything about him seemed to burn, his face, the edges of his hair glistened and seemed to spring off his head, and his eyes were so blue and full of the sun. He looked so young and frail, in spite of the tired line of his mouth. I knew I was taking on more than I was ever likely to be capable of bearing, but there never seemed to be any choice. Well, the howl of outrage and astonishment went up from the family, and that did it. Whether or not he was in love with me, that did it. He made up his mind to marry me.

John Osborne

 1 From the extracts above pick out the words and sentences which you think are:
- the most romantic;
- the least romantic.

Give reasons for your choice.

2 Which character is the more romantic? Why do you think this is so?

a Write *either* Alison's description of their wedding day, *or* Jimmy's description of their first meeting at the party. You need to think about:

- the view of life the character seems to have;
- the sort of words and phrases they usually use;
- the view they are likely to have of this particular situation.

b Create your own imaginary couple, and get them to speak about their relationship. Complete this *either* as a role play exercise, *or* write two monologues.

p152 **c** Is romance an essential part of love? Write your own essay arguing for or against this point.

2 Families

Family relationships, particularly those between parents and children, are never easy, however much love and energy is put into them. Sometimes a poor relationship can ruin the lives of those involved. More frequently the child passes into adulthood with just a slight chip on the shoulder, with a feeling that they were 'hard done by'. This feeling is usually buried, but occasionally surfaces.

On Golden Pond, by Ernest Thompson, is a play about the relationship of Norman and Ethel to their grown-up daughter Chelsea, and her new boyfriend Bill. Below are three extracts from the play. The first is when Chelsea meets her parents after some years away, the second is a conversation between Norman and Bill about sleeping arrangements, and the third follows immediately after Chelsea and her father have had a row. Read the passages through carefully and then answer the questions.

Extract 1:

Chelsea: Mommy. *(They embrace. Quite intensely. Chelsea looks up to Norman, who hasn't moved. She steps to him and hugs him, awkwardly. He is embarrassed, surprised. He hesitates only the briefest instant, then hugs Chelsea.)* Hello, Norman. Happy Birthday.

Norman: Look at you. *(He is touched.)* Look at this little fat girl, Ethel.

Chelsea: *(Stepping back, checks herself, embarrassed.)* Oh, yes. I was going to lose it all and show up skinny, but I was afraid you wouldn't recognise me.

Ethel: You're as thin as a rail. Isn't she Norman?

Norman: Yes. *(There follows a moment of adjustment. Nothing is said. Ethel jumps in quickly.)*

Ethel: Dear Chelsea. I'm so glad you're home.

Chelsea: Oh, God. I thought we'd never get here. We rented a car that explodes every forty miles.

Norman: You rented a car?

Chelsea: Yes, in Boston.

Norman: Huh. What sort of car is it?

Chelsea: Oh, I don't know. Red I think.

Ethel: Ooh! A red car!

Norman: No I meant – what sort of make is it?

Chelsea: Um. I don't know.

Ethel: She doesn't know dear. It doesn't matter.

Norman: Of course it doesn't matter. I was just curious.

Extract 2:

(Billy is Bill's son by another marriage)

Bill: Um. Norman. Um. I don't want to offend you, but there's a rather important little topic that I feel I have to broach.

Norman: *(Looking up)* I beg your pardon?

Bill: I don't want to offend you, but . . . if it's alright with you, we'd like to sleep together.

Norman: What do you mean?

Bill: We'd like to sleep together . . . in the same room . . . in the same bed. If you don't find that offensive.

Norman: All three of you?

Bill: What? Oh no. Just two.

Norman: You and Billy?

Bill: No.

Norman: Not Chelsea and Billy?

Bill: No.

Norman: *(Pausing)* That leaves only Chelsea and you then.

Bill: Yes.

Norman: Why would I find that offensive? You're not planning on doing something unusual, are you?

Bill: Oh, no, just . . . *(He can't go on.)*

Norman: That doesn't seem too offensive, as long as you're quiet.

Extract 3:

Ethel: Can't you be home for five minutes without getting started on the past?

Chelsea: This house seems to set me off.

Ethel: Well it shouldn't. It's a nice house.

Chelsea: I act like a big person everywhere else. I do. I'm in charge of Los Angeles. I guess I've never grown up on Golden Pond. Do you understand?

Ethel: I don't think so.

Chelsea: It doesn't matter. There's just something about coming back here that makes me feel like a little fat girl.

Ethel: Sit down and tell me about your trip.

Chelsea: *(An outburst)* I don't want to sit down. Where were you all that time? You never bailed me out.

Ethel: I didn't know you needed bailing out.

Chelsea: Well, I did.

Ethel: Here we go again. You had a miserable childhood. Your father was overbearing, your mother ignored you. What else is new? Don't you think everyone looks back on their childhood with some bitterness or regret about something? You are a big girl now, aren't you tired of it all? You have this unpleasant chip on your shoulder which is very unattractive. You only come home when I beg you to, and when you get here all you can do is be disagreeable about the past. Life marches by, Chelsea, I suggest you get on with it. *(Ethel stands and glares at Chelsea.)* You're such a nice person. Can't you think of something nice to say?

Ernest Thompson

15

Use the following question as the basis for discussion or writing.

think Which of the following statements do you find to be most true:

Chelsea is headstrong
is selfish
has a chip on her shoulder
is insensitive towards her parents
feels shut out by her parents

Norman likes to feel important
is insensitive
likes embarrassing people
is basically kind-hearted
likes to make jokes

Ethel is sick of Chelsea's complaints
wants to help Chelsea
is the most sensitive character
is the peacemaker

Write down two more phrases appropriate to each character.

choose
a Continue writing one of the scripts.
b Write a prediction of what you think will happen in the play.
c Write an overheard telephone conversation between one of the characters in the sketches, which takes place on the evening after one of the incidents described. It could be:
- Bill describing his awkward conversation with Norman;
- Ethel describing Chelsea's arrival;
- Norman reflecting on this first meeting with Chelsea after several years.

Look at these poems which are written about family relationships.

Love Poem
You are my child
I love you.
I love the roundness of your limbs
Your bottom curves in the palm of my hand.
Where your head ends and your neck begins
Lies a delicious nook
Edged with curls.
Your laughing eyes devour me
Your legs are podgy, sturdy
The dimples in your hands
Dissolve me.
And when the tension mounts,
When the hours of playing, feeding, changing
Watching, waiting
Wear me down . . .
I look at your bonny bottom
And I relent.
You are my child
And I love you.

Ann Hunter

The Children Sleep Soundly Upstairs

He enters
the kitchen.
Purposely he
Brushes against me.
I am infested
with rage.
I want to
paralyse him
With a sharp pair of scissors,
cut him up
like a
feather
pillow
and watch
the stuffing
float into
oblivion.
Broken glass
is spinning
inside
my head.
The children
sleep
soundly
upstairs.

Holly Beeson

think   Use the following questions as the basis for written and oral work.

1   What is it that the mother in the first poem loves about her child?
2   What are the greatest frustrations of parenthood seen in the first poem?
3   Who might the 'he' be in the second poem?
4   What are your reactions to the following phrases:
  ● 'The dimples in your hands dissolve me'
  ● 'Sharp pair of scissors'
  ● 'Broken glass'
5   In what way do the relationships in the two poems differ?

choose   **a**   Make a list of all the nouns, adjectives, or verbs used in one of the poems and then, adding other words of your own, write a poem on another subject.

p159
b   Imagine you are the 'you' in the first poem or the 'he' in the second poem. Write a response to the poem in the form of a letter, monologue or another poem.

c   Write a report which compares and contrasts 'Love Poem' and 'The Children Sleep Soundly Upstairs'. Give your own opinions about the poems as well as giving information.

p161
d   Conduct a survey of the class to find out factual information, or their opinions, on family relationships. Make sure you have a good method of recording the information you receive. Here are some starter questions to help you. You could use these as well as some of your own.

How well do you get on with your brothers and sisters?
1   How many brothers and sisters do you have?
2   Do you share a room?
3   What do you usually disagree about most?
4   What issues do you agree on?

IN THIS CLASS

Have no brothers and sisters.
Have brothers and sisters.

OF THOSE:

Share a room.
Have their own room.

p161 ⇨ Use the information to give an oral or written report on one aspect of family relationships.

> ## Report on Survey.
>
> We conducted a survey in a mixed class of 15 year olds, to find out how people viewed their relationship with their brothers and sisters.

For years people have been fascinated by their ancestors and the environment in which they lived. Read through the following extract which is about one family's background, and then answer the questions.

Jamaica Child

My name is Timothy Macket. I was born and grew up in Jamaica. It was in the country. My parents had a farm, where they grew tobacco, peas and beans. It wasn't a very big farm, but it was enough to keep them busy and bring in the cash. What I liked most about the farm was how from a distance the plants seemed to have evenly grown, but when I came up close it was completely different. Everything was uneven. Sometimes when I had time I used to help plant tobacco, or peas. It was a lot of fun, but hard work. I was nine, and more interested in the river close by the field. The field itself was a long way from home. It was downhill all the way. The field was in a wide, open space. For miles it was green, with trees that rocked from left to right in the midday breeze. There were plants of different types, such as potatoes, tomatoes, and the green long leaves of tobacco. A river divided the wide field into two halves. Footpaths could be seen all around; sometimes they divided a field into sections. Trees of fruits, mangoes, breadfruits and grapes were on the gently sloping hills. Tall fresh green grass surrounded them, but the cows that ploughed the fields would trample over it as they ate in the evenings.

The workers who helped in the field started early so that they could get a lot finished before the sun's heat became unbearable. When the sun became hot, the people would get irritable and short tempered.

As far back as I can remember, I used to help on the field, not that I was much of a help. I was perhaps more a nuisance at my age than a help. The neighbours were kind to me, they came into our yard to see my mother. They would be there for what seemed to me like hours. They would be laughing one minute, then all of a sudden they would be disagreeing with each other.

Erol O'Connor

19

think **1** Give a short, factual description of the part of Jamaica which Timothy describes.
      2 What aspects of the environment do you think you would like and dislike?

The information in the story comes, in this case, from the writer's memory. Information can also be gleaned by talking to relatives, reading diaries, and filling in the gaps by looking at text books and official records.

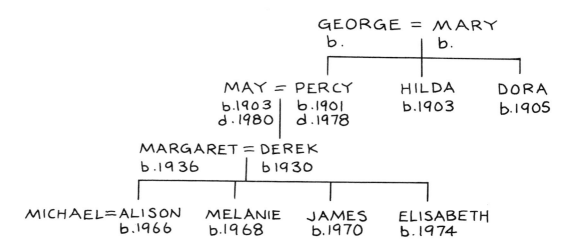

choose **a** Use as many of the above as you can to compile your own family tree.
       b Write a brief biography of your own family's development. You may choose to write about your own generation or about generations past.
       c Find out as much as you can about one of your relatives from another generation. The account below, from Miss Read's book, *The Fortunate Grandchild*, may give you some ideas.

She was my mother's mother and must have been nearly seventy when I first became conscious of her in about 1915. At that time, my father was serving in France with H Battery of the Royal Horse Artillery, and my mother was carrying on his job as an insurance agent. My elder sister and I were left with Grandma Read, who lived nearby, for most of the day.

She was small and neat, with a very smooth skin and dark hair parted in the middle and taken back behind her ears into a bun. Her hair remained dark and glossy until her death at seventy-six. It was generally believed that she had a Portuguese forbear and her looks would certainly bear this out.

She dressed well. Her frocks were of dark silk, usually brown or black, trimmed with lace and made with a high neck. She was particularly fond of prettily-trimmed bonnets worn tied under the chin with ribbons. As children, we often gave her bonnet trimmings of feathers or velvet for her birthday or Christmas presents. One particular bonnet I remember clearly, trimmed with velvet pansies of different colours which framed her face and delighted my admiring eye.

An older cousin of mine remembers her as 'a very happy lady. She had a nice smile, and her eyes smiled too.' That too is how I remember her.

She was a wonderful companion to young children, cheerful, spritely and not over-anxious, as so many adults are, about the niceties of correct behaviour or the awful consequences of such daring feats as jumping off low walls or down the conservatory steps. Having had twelve children of her own, she was probably past worrying over much.

She indulged me in small ways, and I loved her for it.

During that war, food supplies were extremely short, especially in London. My mother had instilled in us that we were never to ask for sweets, or anything with sugar in it because people had so little. My grandmother, however, would frequently spread butter – or more probably margarine in those dark days – on half a slice of bread, and then scatter brown sugar on it. I watched greedily as she cut it into fingers which I soon demolished. I knew, as well as she did, that this activity was only undertaken when we were alone, and I had enough sense, even at three, to keep our secret.

Miss Read

3 Partings

When a relationship ends due to misunderstanding the wounds take a long time to heal. Below are three poems which describe a relationship ending. Read them through carefully and then answer the questions.

A Blade of Grass

You ask for a poem,
I offer you a blade of grass.
You say it is not good enough.
You ask for a poem.

I say this blade of grass will do.
It has dressed itself in frost,
It is more immediate
Than any image of my making.

You say it is not a poem
It is a blade of grass and grass
Is not quite good enough.
I offer you a blade of grass.

You are indignant.
You say it is too easy to offer grass.
It is absurd.
Anyone can offer a blade of grass.

You ask for a poem.
And so I write you a tragedy about
How a blade of grass
Becomes more and more difficult to offer,

And about how as you grow older
A blade of grass
Becomes more and more difficult to accept.

Brian Patten

Declaration of Intent

She said she'd
love me for eternity
but managed to reduce
it to eight months
for good behaviour.
She said we fitted
like a hand in a glove
but then the hot
weather came and such
accessories weren't needed.
She said the future
was ours but the deeds
were made out in
her name.
She said I was
the only one who
understood completely

and then she left me
and said she knew
that I'd understand completely.

Steve Turner

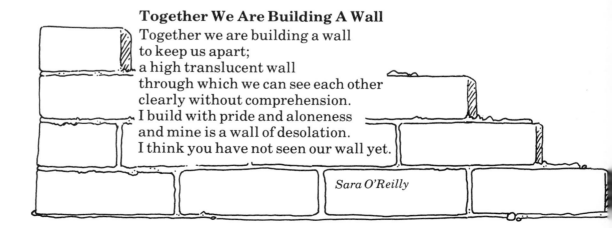

Together We Are Building A Wall

Together we are building a wall
to keep us apart;
a high translucent wall
through which we can see each other
clearly without comprehension.
I build with pride and aloneness
and mine is a wall of desolation.
I think you have not seen our wall yet.

Sara O'Reilly

think

choose

Pick out one sentence from each poem which sums up the ideas of the poem, or which you found particularly striking.

a All three poems use repetition effectively. The first poem repeats 'a blade of grass' to stress how often it is offered and refused. The second poem repeats 'a wall' to stress their separation. Write your own poem about the end of a relationship using the technique of repetition.

b The poem 'Declaration of Intent', although not funny, does make the reader smile through its picking apart of romantic phrases:
- 'love me for eternity'
- 'fitted like a hand in a glove'
- 'the future was ours'
- 'the only one who understood completely.'

followed by unromantic ideas:
- 'managed to reduce it to eight months for good behaviour.'

Write your own poem or passage which makes fun of conventional images of love.

The following poem and article are linked in that they look at relationships which have ended in death, but there are other links too. See how many similarities you can find between them as you read through.

From *A Death in Winter*
Beside the exit, seated at a table
is a grey clerk with a ledger
At his feet is a kind of box
a trunk perhaps, a hope chest or
a rubbish bin.

Cross-legged in the doorway
my friend sits, watching light
stream in through the opening.
It soaks her in beauty.

She has given back her future.
In character, neatly folded, she placed it in the box
and the clerk ticked it off.
Now she takes off her feet, like shoes
gently, one beside the other;
she takes her speech and returns it
syllable by syllable
she unpicks it thoughtfully, like knitting
unravels it, one plain, one purl
meaning by meaning;
she gives back her hands –
lays them down in the box with a smile.
There is no regret in her
She knows their excellence.
And now she gives back her continence, choices, understanding the strange
comings and goings about her.
Everything she returns is fine and cared for
The clerk ticks it all of in his ledger.

She is hardly human now
she is almost entirely love
she has given back her children
a very little of the personal
is left in her heart.

To the left of the doorway is a linen basket.
A plump girl, laughing, kneels beside it.
She is handing out gifts
to the souls who come trooping
in through the opening like sunlight.

Hands to grip a finger
feet to walk
the first smile
Mama, Papa, I want, I think
all the trappings of the journey.

My friend smiles across at the girl
as if she were a daughter.

The radiance streams in and over her
soon she will take off the last of her body
and step out into the stillness.

Jeni Couzyn

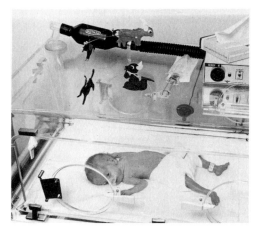

Little Nicola Bell was born almost two months early. She had been expected this weekend but three months ago her mother Deborah suffered a massive brain haemorrhage. Although clinically dead, her body was kept alive in a ventilator machine until Nicola could be delivered by Caesarian section, five weeks later. Her father Ian explained: 'I'd heard the heartbeat, seen it kick. I felt that if they turned the machine off, they would be killing the baby. And I wouldn't want another life lost.'

But it almost was. In the first weeks of her life, the little scrap of humanity — weighing less than a sugar bag — endured jaundice, anaemia and a serious chest infection.

It is only now that Ian can bear to talk about the night when Dr Peter Morrell, the consultant paediatrician at Middlesbrough Maternity Hospital, phoned him at work to warn that Nicola had suffered a grave setback.

As he watched over her in the baby care unit willing her to make it, Ian thinks he was probably the most optimistic person there: 'Afterwards they told me that although she had already been called a miracle baby the real miracle was that she had survived that night.'

The care of the doctors and nurses saved her. They monitored her every function, feeding her dextrose and breast milk from the hospital milk bank, keeping her on a mineral and amino-acid drip.

Today Ian feels he can afford to be truly optimistic. And his mother, Mrs Kathleen Bell, prepares to welcome Nicola into the home where Ian grew up.

'She'll be having my old room,' Ian said. 'The shifts I work will mean I'll have either every morning or afternoon with her and I intend to make the most of her.

She is everything. When the time is right I'll tell her what a lovely mother she had.'

YOU Magazine

1 Pick out two images used in the poem to describe a person's death.
2 Describe in your own words what happens to the 'she' in the poem.
3 Why do you think there is 'no regret in her'?
4 What were the two most dangerous times for baby Nicola Bell?
5 Which of the following do you think is the most true. The common link between the poem and the article is:

- people dying;
- the people who mourn;
- the dead living on in our memories;
- life after death;
- people dying young.

p163 ▷

a Write a review of 'Death in Winter'. You will need to include:

- the ideas put across in the poem;
- the vocabulary used;
- the images created through comparison.

b Write your own poem or description of someone who has died.
c Death is normally seen as a very pessimistic time, but in the two extracts it is seen as less final. Choose your own subject which people normally see as negative and place it in a more positive light.

---

extra Love

The following passage is an extract from a short story called *The Valentine Generation* by John Wain. Read it through carefully and then answer the questions which follow.

'Don't you believe in love?' she asks.

'Well as a matter of fact I do,' I say. 'I got married myself, soon after I joined the post office, and I can't believe I'd have been as happy with anyone else as I have been with my wife. I did all right when I picked her out. But that was back in the days when marriages were made to last. Everything's different with you young people today.'

'You think so?' she says. 'Really different?'

'Course it is,' I say. 'All the romance has gone out of it. Well, look at it. Sex, sex, sex from morning to night and never a bit of sentiment.'

'What's wrong with sex?' she says, looking stubborn.

'Nothing,' I say, 'only in my day we didn't try to build a fire with nothing but kindling.'

I turn away, thinking I'll leave her to chew that one over. I'm just getting the van door open when suddenly she's there, grabbing at my wrist.

'Please,' she says. 'Please. You've got a kind face. I know you'd help me if only you knew.'

'All right,' I say, 'but make it fast. And don't kid yourself that I'll give you the letter when you've finished.' I meant it too. Regulations mean a lot after forty years.

'I usually spend Saturday evening with Jocelyn,' she begins. Jocelyn. I don't like the sound that. 'And last Saturday, that's the day before yesterday, he rings up and tells me he can't do it. He's got to look after his aunt who's coming up from the country. So when my brother and sister-in-law happened to look in and see me, I said I'd go out with them for the evening. We went up to the West End and I said I'd show them a nice little restaurant I knew. So we went into this place and the very first person I saw was Jocelyn.'

'With his aunt from the country,' I say.

'His aunt from the country,' she says, nodding and looking very grim. 'About twenty years old with a lot of red hair and a dress cut very low. And there was Jocelyn, leaning towards her the way he does when he's really interested in a girl.'

'What a surprise for him,' I say.

'No surprise,' she says. 'He never saw me. I knew at once I wouldn't be able to stand it. I wasn't going to have a show down with him there and then, and as for sitting down and watching the performance and trying to eat my dinner with my brother and his wife there on top of everything else as well.'

'So you ducked out quick, and came home and wrote him a nasty letter,' I say. Nine o'clock news creeping up and I'm ruddy nowhere with my collecting.

'After that,' she says, 'I go home and spend a completely sleepless night. I don't even close my eyes, because every time I close them I see Jocelyn's face as he leans towards the girl.'

'All right, let him lean.' I say 'If he's the type that runs after every bit of skirt he sees, he won't make you happy anyway.'

'But he does make me happy,' she says. 'He's absolutely ideal for me. He makes me feel marvellous. When I'm with him I'm really glad about being a woman.'

'Even if you don't trust him?' I ask.

'Casual infidelities don't matter,' she says. 'It's the really deep communication between man and woman that matters.'

'Listen to me, miss,' I say. 'Take an old man's advice and leave that letter where it is. If it puts an end to this business between you and this Jocelyn bloke, believe me, you'll live to be grateful.'

At that she stares at me as if she's caught me doing something so horrible she can't trust her own eyesight.

'It's unbelievable,' she says at last. 'If any body had told me that – that ordinary human beings were capable of such stupidity and cruelty, yes, cruelty, I wouldn't have believed them.' And she begins to cry, quite silently, with the tears running down her nose.

'Which of us is cruel?' I ask her. 'Me or Jocelyn?'

'You, of course,' she says, so cross at what she thinks is cheek on my part that she stops crying. 'You're making me miserable for ever, just so that you won't have to admit that your ideas of love are out of date and wrong.'

'Whereas Jocelyn is sweetness and kindness itself, eh?' I put in.

'No of course not,' she says. 'He's capable of hardness and aggressiveness and he can be cruel himself at times. That's all part of his being a real man, the sort of man who can make a girl feel good about being feminine.' That's another bit of Jocelyn's patter, if I'm any judge.

'A man who was sweetness and kindness itself,' she goes on, bringing out the words as if they're choking her, 'wouldn't be capable of making a woman feel fulfilled and happy. He's got to have a streak of . . . of . . .'

'Of the jungle in him?' I say, trying to help her out.

'If you like, yes,' she says, nodding and looking solemn.

'Well, I don't like it,' I say, letting it rip

for once. 'I think you're a nice girl, but you're being very silly. You've let this Jocelyn stuff your head full of silly ideas, you've taken his word for it that he can chase every bit of skirt he meets, tell lies to you, string you along every inch of the way, and it doesn't matter because he's going to make you feel happy and relaxed, he's going to make you feel good about being a woman because he's Tarzan of the flipping Apes. Go and find some young man who'll tell you that as a woman you deserve to be cherished and taken care of. Who'll love you enough to tell you the truth and play fair with you. Even if he isn't an animal out of the zoo. Make do with an ordinary human being,' I say to her. 'You'll find it cheaper in the long run.'

'Why . . .' she begins, but she's crying too much to talk. I wait a bit and she has another go and this time it comes out. 'Why are you so sure that you know best and that I must be wrong?' She asks me. 'Well, it's simple,' I say. 'I've had a happy marriage for nearly forty years. So naturally I know how they work. I know what you have to do.'

'But love changes!' she says, bringing it out as if she's struggling for words that'll convince me. 'I'm sure you've been happy, but you're wrong if you think that your way of being happy would work for young people today. You belong to a different generation.'

John Wain

think

1 What is the difference between the postman's idea of love and the girl's love for Jocelyn?

2 What does she mean by 'casual infidelities don't matter'?

3 Is the love experienced by young people usually different from that experienced by older people?

4 In what ways can the love between two people change as they grow older?

choose

a 'You're wrong if you think your way of being happy would work for young people today.' Does love change from generation to generation? Is the concept of love held by the postman inappropriate for young people today? Write a report on your views on this.

b If you had been the postman, what advice would you have given to the girl and what sort of arguments would you have used? Would you have given the letter back to her? Write your own letter of advice to the girl in the story.

 p156

c Write an essay with one of the following titles:
   ● What I look for in a partner
   ● Love at first sight

d This passage is only an extract taken from the centre of a short story. Build up the rest of the story, before and after the extract, to make your own short story. You need to consider:
   ● *The style of writer* – The sentence length, choice of vocabulary, use of images, and position of the narrator.
   ● *The characters* – How have they reacted so far? How does their manner of speaking differ? How do their lifestyles differ?
   ● *The plot* – What has happened so far? What do you think will happen next? What happened immediately before the passage?

You might find it useful to talk about these points before you write.

starter | **Why I write**

You probably spend a great deal of your school career writing, but have you ever wondered why you are writing and who you are writing for?

Why do I write?

Who am I writing for?

Reasons for writing and the audience for whom it is intended are very closely connected. In school you may often feel that *wanting* to write is the last reason for doing so, and that writing for yourself is the most unlikely audience. Yet, *professional* writers often have that as their highest motivation. This is particularly true of novelists and poets, but also true of other writers such as journalists, lawyers and teachers.

Very often the reasons you write in school are:

- because it helps you to *remember* something (a Science experiment);
- because it *clarifies* your views on something (a History essay);
- because it allows you to use your *imagination* (English creative writing).

p146 **1** Make a list of the different pieces of writing you have written today, or on any given day. Then decide what type of writing each piece is.

choose **a** Complete a piece of writing which fulfils one of the functions above of remembering, clarifying or imagining. Decide on the particular audience it is intended for and angle the writing to please that audience. Think, for instance, how you might write differently for:

- your parents;
- your teacher;
- your friends;
- the class.

Present it to that audience and ask them for their views on it, then refine the writing, if necessary, so that it satisfies the audience.

b Write a story which *you* want to write, which has *you* as the target audience. When you have finished, look at it very critically and then rework it until you are really pleased with it.

c Write one of the following, paying particular attention to the *audience* for whom it is intended.

- A news report of a fire in an Old People's Home, which will be read by old people in other homes to reassure them of the overall safety of their home.
- A letter to the government complaining about one of its most recent decisions.
- A short story for an eight-year-old.

1

Writers

The following extracts, written by George Orwell, begin to investigate reasons for writing. Orwell was writing in the 1930s and 1940s and his best known novels are *Animal Farm* and *1984*, both of which consider the political systems which operate in our society. He also wrote several books about poverty and working conditions. Read through the extracts carefully and then answer the questions.

Why I write

From a very early age, perhaps the age of five or six, I knew that when I grew up I should be a writer. Between the ages of about seventeen and twenty-four I tried to abandon this idea, but I did so with the consciousness that I was outraging my true nature that sooner or later I should have to settle down and write books.

I was the middle child of three, but there was a gap of five years on either side, and I barely saw my father before I was eight. For this and other reasons I was somewhat lonely, and I soon developed disagreeable mannerisms which made me unpopular throughout my schooldays. I had the lonely child's habit of making up stories and holding conversations with imaginary persons, and I think from the very start my literary ambitions were mixed up with the feeling of being isolated and undervalued. I knew that I had a facility with words and a power of facing unpleasant facts, and I felt that this created a sort of private world in which I could get my own back for my failure in everyday life . . .

Later in the book he outlines four different reasons why people write:

1. Sheer egoism. Desire to seem clever, to be talked about, to be remembered after death, to get your own back on grownups who snubbed you in childhood etc. . .

2. Aesthetic enthusiasm. Perception of beauty in the external world, or, on the other hand, in words and their arrangement . . . Desire to share an experience which one feels is valuable and ought not to be missed.

3. Historical impulse. Desire to see things as they are, to find out true facts and store them up for the use of posterity.

4. Political purpose – using the word 'political' in the widest possible sense. Desire to push the world in a certain direction, to alter other people's idea of the kind of society that they should strive after . . .

George Orwell

 1 What led George Orwell to begin his writing?
2 Orwell gives four reasons for writing, explain them in your own words.

 **a** Looking carefully at Orwell's four motives for writing, and, having put them into your own words, think of some more from your own experience of writing. Then write an essay entitled 'Why I write'.

p161 ⇨

p152 ▷ **b** In what ways can schools alter their courses to suit Orwell's motives for writing; and *if* they can *should they*? Write your own argumentative essay on this subject.

c Do you think it takes a particular type of person to be a professional writer or can anyone do it? What do you see as the qualities of a good writer? Imagine you are running a newspaper and you are looking for a good writer. Complete a role play of the meeting at which your company decides what is needed in a good writer. Write an advertisement for a local paper stating the qualities you see as necessary for the p174 ▷ job. Having completed the advertisement, conduct the interview between the newspaper and the writer.

2 Short stories

Below is an essay written by Adèle Geras, discussing the particular mode of writing known as the short story. Read it through carefully and then compare it with the list which follows.

Every short story is unique: one of a kind. Every short story presents its writer with new problems and the short stories you've written in the past are generally of little help. There are, of course, broad categories of story: after you've written a few, you can probably say into which categories your own stories fall and which kind you most enjoy writing. Let me list a few:

1. The story as an extended anecdote/joke with a strong punch-line or a dramatic twist in the tail.
2. The story as a glimpse through a window, a small slice of a largely unknown life.
3. The 'what if?' story. A great deal of horror and science fiction writing falls into this category. Take an idea, the author thinks, and stretch it as far as it'll go without snapping.
4. The prose poem. This is usually an extended description, perhaps of a landscape, to convey a feeling or evoke a mood.
5. The character study. This is a glimpse through a microscope at one person in often quite absorbing detail.
6. The 'Ancient Mariner' type. These stories are always in the first person,

with a strong author's voice speaking directly to you and not letting you move till the story is over. Damon Runyan was an American writer of the 1930s who wrote of small time crooks, not-very-efficient gamblers and their assorted lady friends in such an individual way that you can almost 'hear' the words on the page. How's this for a first sentence? It comes from a story called 'Tobias the Terrible':

'One night I am sitting in Mindy's restaurant on Broadway partaking heartily of some Hungarian goulash which comes very nice in Mindy's, what with the chef being personally somewhat Hungarian himself, when in pops a guy who is a stranger to me and sits at my table.'

7. The small drama. This is more like a short play than anything else. Something happens to someone, someone does something, feels something, says something to another person, and some kind of change or resolution is achieved.

The last word for anyone who wants to write. Look at everything. Listen to people as they speak, watch the way they

move. Read everything you can lay
hands on. Be honest. Tell it like it is for
you, even if (especially if) it's the most
way-out fantasy. Try out voices.
Improvise on paper. Try and write
something every day, as if writing were a
muscle that needed exercise. The
greatest story in the world is nothing
locked up inside your head. *Write it down
now*. Then put your feet up!

Adèle Geras

Some Aspects of Short Stories
simple characters
a twist at the end
a fast moving story line
a moral/a lesson to be learnt
a good idea
a strong sense of setting
short sentences
an easy to read, conversational style
a clear plot
an idea that sets you thinking
characters who are described in terms of their looks/easy to imagine
a plot which is divided into episodes
no interference from the author
vocabulary which is easy to understand
short paragraphs

1 Above are some factors you often find in short stories. Read them through carefully and then list them in order of importance to a good short story.

2 Read through one of the following short stories which can be found in other units in this book: *Elethia* (on page 41), *The Pedestrian* by Ray Bradbury (on page 98), *Late Home* by Trevor Millum (on page 108).

a Which of the characteristics, described by Adèle Geras or mentioned in the list which follows her essay, are used in the story you have chosen? Write down your findings in a brief informative piece of writing.

p161 ▷

b Decide on the most important elements for a short story. Then write one of your own which combines these elements. You will need to choose your *genre* (science fiction, murder mystery, romance) your characters, and your setting in time and space. Then you will need to decide:

p159 ▷

- Are you narrating as a character in the story?
- Are you a narrator standing outside the story?
- Are you just the writer standing outside the story itself?

c   Some short stories are extremely short. The following are mini-sagas; stories of fifty words exactly.

Mirror eyes at the doctors
She was with her dog: it was her turn next. She looked in the mirror and found in horror that she was her dog and her dog was her.
'Next please.'
The dog went in and closed the door. She heard him say: 'I haven't been feeling quite myself.'

Tom Bilton

What the Sleeping Beauty would have given her right arm for
This princess was different. She was a brunette beauty with a genius of a brain. Refusing marriage, she inherited all by primogenesis. The country's economy prospered under her rule. When the handsome prince came by on his white charger, she bought it from him and started her own racehorse business.

Zoe Ellis

Homecoming
'Good to have you back, son,' the old man said.
'Nice to be back.'
'You've had a rough time.' The eyes clouded with guilt. 'Hope you don't think I let you down.'
The younger shook his head. 'You warned me, dad. But it wasn't the nails. It was the kiss.'

Roger Wodis

The final punishment
God saw that the earth was evil so God sent forth a pestilence.
A curse to punish the earth for once and all.
A curse that would infect land after land like a disease, and spread through-out the Globe like a forest fire.
For this curse would be named, Man.

Nathan Williams

i)   From the stories above, talk about and decide which of the seven types of story (according to Adèle Geras' definitions) has been written in each case.

ii) Which mini-saga do you find the most enjoyable or interesting? Why?

iii) *Either:*
   ● Write your own mini-saga of exactly fifty words. It must tell a complete story. You could try to summarize a soap opera into fifty words.
   or:
   ● Rewrite the short story you chose to read earlier as a fifty word mini-saga.

3   **Personal writing**

The following extract is taken from *The Diary of Anne Frank*. Anne Frank later died in a German concentration camp. Read it through carefully and then look at the list of information about Anne Frank which is written under **Facts** and **Impressions**.

Saturday, 20th June, 1942

I haven't written for a few days, because I wanted first of all to think about my diary. It's an odd idea for someone like me to keep a diary; not only because I have never done so before, but because it seems to me that neither I – nor for that matter anyone else – will be interested in the unbosomings of a thirteen-year-old schoolgirl. Still, what does that matter? I want to write, but more than that, I want to bring out all kinds of things that lie buried deep in my heart.

There is a saying that 'paper is more patient than man'; it came back to me on one of my slightly melancholy days, while I sat chin in hand, feeling too bored and limp even to make up my mind whether to go out or to stay at home. Yes, there is no doubt that paper is patient and as I don't intend to show this cardboard-covered notebook, bearing the proud name of 'diary', to anyone, unless I find a real friend, boy or girl, probably nobody cares. And now I come to the root of the matter, the reason for my starting a diary: it is that I have no such real friend.

Let me put it more clearly, since no one will believe that a girl of thirteen feels herself quite alone in the world, nor is it so. I have darling parents and a sister of sixteen. I know about thirty people whom one might call friends – I have strings of boy friends, anxious to catch a glimpse of me and who, failing that, peep at me through mirrors in class. I have relations, aunts and uncles, who are darlings too, a good home, no – I don't seem to lack anything. But it's the same with all my friends, just fun and games, nothing more. I can never bring myself to talk of anything outside the common round. We don't seem to be able to get any closer, that is the root of the trouble. Perhaps I lack confidence, but anyway, there it is, a stubborn fact and I don't seem to be able to do anything about it. Hence, this diary. In order to enhance in my mind's eye the picture of the friend for whom I have waited so long, I don't want to set down a series of bald facts in a diary like most people do, but I want this diary itself to be my friend, and I shall call my friend Kitty. No one will grasp what I'm talking about if I begin my letters to Kitty just out of the blue, so, albeit unwillingly, I will start by sketching in brief the story of my life.

My father was 36 when he married my mother, who was then 25. My sister Margot was born in 1926 in Frankfort-on-Main. I followed on 12th June, 1929, and, as we are Jewish, we emigrated to Holland in 1933, where my father was appointed Managing Director of Travies N.V. This firm is in close relationship with the firm of Kolen & Co. in the same building, of which my father is a partner

The rest of our family, however, felt the full impact of Hitler's anti-Jewish laws, so life was filled with anxiety. In 1938 after the pogroms, my two uncles (my mother's brothers) escaped to the U.S.A. My old grandmother came to us, she was then 73. After May, 1940, good times rapidly fled: first the war, then the capitulation, followed by the arrival of the Germans. That is when the sufferings of us Jews really began. Anti-Jewish decrees followed each other in quick succession. Jews must wear a yellow star, Jews must hand in their bicycles, Jews are banned from trams and are forbidden to drive. Jews are only allowed to do their shopping between three and five o'clock and then only in shops which bear the placard 'Jewish shop'. Jews must be indoors by eight o'clock and cannot even sit in their own gardens after that hour. Jews are forbidden to visit theatres, cinemas, and other places of entertainment. Jews may not take part in public sports. Swimming baths, tennis courts, hockey fields, and other sports grounds are all prohibited to them. Jews may not visit Christians. Jews must go to Jewish schools, and many more restrictions of a similar kind.

So we could not do this and were forbidden to do that. But life went on in spite of it all. Jopie used to say to me: 'You're scared to do anything, because it may be forbidden.' Our freedom was strictly limited. Yet things were still bearable.

Granny died in January, 1942; no one will ever know how much she is present in my thoughts and how much I love her still.

In 1934 I went to school at the Montessori Kindergarten and continued there. It was at the end of the school year, I was in form 6B, when I had to say good-bye to Mrs. K.

Saturday, 20th June, 1942

Dear Kitty,

I'll start straight away. It is so peaceful at the moment, Mummy and Daddy are out and Margot has gone to play ping-pong with some friends.

I've been playing ping-pong a lot myself lately. We ping-pongers are very partial to an ice-cream, especially in summer when one gets warm at the game, so we usually finish up with a visit to the nearest ice-cream shop, 'Delphi' or 'masis', where Jews are allowed. We've given up scrounging for extra pocket money. 'Oasis' is usually full and amongst our large circle of friends we always manage to find some kind-hearted gentleman or boy friend, who presents us with more ice-cream than we could devour in a week.

I expect you will be rather surprised at the fact that I should talk of boy friends at my age. Alas, one simply can't seem to avoid it at our school. As soon as a boy asks if he may cycle home with me and we get into conversation, nine out of ten times I can be sure that he will fall head over heels in love immediately and simply won't allow me out of his sight. After a while it cools down of course,

especially as I take little notice of ardent looks and pedal blithely on.

If it gets so far that they begin about 'asking Father' I swerve slightly on my bicycle, my satchel falls, the young man is bound to get off and hand it to me, by which time I have introduced a new topic of conversation.

These are the most innocent types; you get some who blow kisses or try to get hold of your arm, but then they are definitely knocking at the wrong door. I get off my bicycle and refuse to go farther in their company, or I pretend to be insulted and tell them in no uncertain terms to clear off.

There, the foundation of our friendship is laid, till tomorrow!

Yours, ANNE.
Anne Frank

35

Facts

Anne:

is thirteen years-old
wants to write
has no real friends
has two parents
has a sister of sixteen
writes to her diary in place of a friend
is clever
calls her diary Kitty
is Jewish
moved to Holland in 1933
her father is a businessman
wider family persecuted by the Germans
restricted during the war because Jewish
grandmother died five months before diary entry

Impressions

is sometimes melancholy/sad
sometimes gets bored
popular with the boys
pretty
very attached to her grandmother
longs for a close friend
very close to her family
uncertain of herself

The following extract is taken from a diary published as a book called *Go Ask Alice*. Alice is a drug addict who eventually dies of her addiction.

December 31

Tonight will ring in a wonderful new year for me. How humbly grateful I am to be rid of the old one. It hardly seems real! I wish I could just tear it out of my life like pages from the calendar, at least the last six months. How, oh how, could it ever have happened to me? Me, from this good and fine and upstanding, loving family! But the new year is going to be different, filled with life and promise. I wish there were some way to literally and truly and completely and permanently blot my for-real nightmares out, but since there isn't, I must poke them way back into the darkest and most inaccessible corners and crevices of my brain, where perhaps they will eventually be covered over or become lost.

January 24

Oh damn, damn, damn, it's happened again. I don't know whether to scream with glory or cover myself with sackcloth whatever that means. Anyone who says pot and acid are not addicting is a damn stupid, raving idiot, unenlightened fool! I've been on them since July 10, and when I've been off I've been scared to death to even think of anything that even looks or seems like dope. All the time pretending to myself that I could take it or leave it.

Write down all the information you can glean about the person of Alice, under **Facts** and **Impressions**.

p154 ▷

a Write a description of Anne or Alice from another person's point of view. It could be:
  - a parent;
  - a friend;
  - an associate (e.g. a drug pusher in the second extract), or just a person who has heard of their deaths.

b Both Anne and Alice died soon after their diaries were written, and yet you do not get the impression that they were aware of their oncoming fate. Write the diary entry you think one of them might have written, had they been aware of the fact that they would die the next day.

c Write your own diary for a week, in the style of one of the diaries above.

Read through the following fictitious extracts and write a list of information about the person who is supposed to have written them, dividing your information into **Facts** and **Impressions**.

The Catcher in the Rye

If you really want to hear about it, the first thing you'll probably want to know is where I was born, and what my lousy childhood was like, and how my parents were occupied and all before they had me, and all that David Copperfield kind of crap, but I don't feel like going into it. In the first place, that stuff bores me, and in the second place, my parents would have about two haemorrhages a piece if I told anything pretty personal about them. They're quite touchy about anything like that, especially my father. They're *nice* and all – I'm not saying that – but they're also touchy as hell. Besides, I'm not going to tell you my whole goddam autobiography or anything. I'll just tell you about this madman stuff that happened to me around last Christmas before I got pretty run-down and had to come out here and take it easy.

J.D. Salinger

Great Expectations

My father's family name being Pirrip, and my Christian name Philip, my infant tongue could make of both names nothing longer or more explicit than Pip. So, I called myself Pip, and came to be called Pip.

I give Pirrip as my father's name, on the authority of his tombstone and my sister – Mrs Joe Gargery, who married the blacksmith. As I never saw my father or my mother, and never saw any likeness of either of them (for their days were long before the days of photographs), my first fancies regarding what they were like, were unreasonably derived from their tombstones. The shape of the letters on my father's, gave me an odd idea that he was a square, stout, dark man with curly black hair. From the character and turn of the inscription, *'Also Georgiana wife of the above'*, I drew a childish conclusion that my mother was freckled and sickly.

Charles Dickens

The Secret Diary of Adrian Mole

Thursday January 1st
BANK HOLIDAY IN ENGLAND, IRELAND, SCOTLAND AND WALES.
These are my New Year's resolutions:
1   I will help the blind across the road.
2   I will hang my trousers up.
3   I will put the sleeves back on my records.
4   I will not start smoking.
5   I will stop squeezing my spots.
6   I will be kind to the dog.
7   I will help the poor and ignorant.
8   After hearing the disgusting noises from downstairs last night, I have also vowed never to drink alcohol.

Sue Townsend

1   In what way do the imagined writers differ from each other in terms of:
   ● their experience of life;
   ● their character;
   ● where they are living?

choose

Now use the information you have gleaned to complete one of the following assignments.

a Write another 300 words to continue one of the extracts, taking care to imitate the way in which the character writes, and checking that you do not contradict the information you have already been given. You will need to use your imagination to fill in any gaps in the information.

b Write a diary for a fictitious character of your own making.

c Write your own diary, in your own style, for at least one week. It needs to be a record of some of the things you've done; a catalogue of your views and reflections on those events; and a place where you are honest about thoughts and feelings.

extra Looking at an author through their writing

To learn about an author you must read their work, and read it closely. Of course it is a good idea to read their longer pieces of writing but you can also learn a great deal, particularly about their style, from short stories.

Below are extracts from three short stories and one complete story written by two writers, Alice Walker and Stan Barstow. Take time to read them carefully and then answer the questions which follow.

The Desperadoes

What started it that night was the row Vince had with his father. He couldn't remember just what began the row itself, but something like it seemed to blow up every time the Old Man saw him, and started using expressions like 'idle layabout', 'lazy good-for-nothing' and 'no-good little teddy boy'. The Old Man never talked to you – he talked at you; he didn't carry on a conversation – he told you things. When Vince stormed out of the house he hardly knew where he was going he was so full of bottled-up fury.

Violence writhed in him like a trapped and vicious snake. He felt like kicking in the teeth of the first person who might glance twice at him and he thought that perhaps the easiest way of relieving his feelings would be to find the boys and go smash up a few chairs at the Youth Club. Except that that might bring a copper to the door and he got on the wrong side of the Old Man easily enough without having the police to help along.

He had no trouble in finding the gang: they were obstructing the pavement at the end of Chapel Street, making the occasional passer-by get off into the road. He watched them sourly as he descended the hill – stocky Sam, little Finch, and big surly Bob – and his mouth twisted peevishly as he heard one of them laugh. They were watching something across the road that he could not see and they did not notice his approach till he was upon them.

'Now then.'

'What ho!'

'How do, Vince.'

Sam said, 'Get a load of that,' nodding across the junction.

Vince looked. He might have known. It was a girl. She was straddling a drop-handlebar bicycle by the kerb and talking to a thin youth who stood on the edge of the pavement. She was a dark blonde. She wore very brief scarlet shorts which displayed her long, handsome thighs, and a white high-necked sweater stretched tight over her large shapely breasts.

Finch was hopping about as though taken bad for a leak and making little growling noises in his throat.

'D'you know her?' Vince asked.

'Never seen her before.'

'Who's that Sunday-school teacher with her?'

'Don't know him either.'

Vince felt a spasm of gratuitous hatred for the youth. There was nobody about; the street was quiet in the early evening. He said, 'Well, what we waitin' for? Let's see him off, eh?'

'An' what then?' Bob said.

Vince looked at him where he lounged against the lamp-post, his hands deep in the pockets of his black jeans. He was becoming more and more irritated by Bob's habit of making objections to everything he suggested. He had a strong idea that Bob fancied taking over leadership of the gang but lacked the guts to force the issue.

'What d'you mean "what then?"?' he said.

There was no expression on Bob's long sullen face. 'When we've seen him off?'

'We'll take her pants off an' make her ride home bare-back,' Finch giggled.

'Aye,' Vince said; 'an' if laughing boy has any objections we'll carve his initials round his belly button.'

He brought his hand out of his pocket and pushed the handle of his knife against Bob's shirt front just above the buckle of his belt. He pressed the catch and let his relaxed wrist take the spring of the blade. He wondered if anyone had ever made a knife with a spring strong enough to drive the blade straight into a man's belly.

'You want to be careful wi' that bloody thing,' Bob said, eyeing the six inches of razor-sharp steel, its point pricking one of the pearl buttons on his black shirt. 'Don't you know there's a law against 'em?'

'I'll have to be careful who sees me with it, then, won't I?' Vince said. Looking Bob in the eye he inclined his head across the street. 'Comin'?' he said.

Bob shrugged with exaggerated casualness and eased his shoulders away from the lamp-post as Vince retracted the blade of the knife. 'Okay; may as well.'

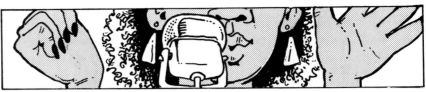

1955

The car is a brandnew red Thunderbird convertible, and it's passed the house more than once. It slows down real slow now, and stops at the curb. An older gentleman dressed like a Baptist deacon gets out on the side near the house, and a young fellow who looks about sixteen gets out on the driver's side. They are white, and I wonder what in the world they doing in this neighborhood.

Well, I say to J.T., put your shirt on, anyway, and let me clean these glasses offa the table.

We had been watching the ballgame on TV. I wasn't actually watching, I was sort of daydreaming, with my foots up in J.T.'s lap.

I seen 'em coming on up the walk, brisk, like they coming to sell something, and then they rung the bell, and J.T. declined to put on a shirt but instead disappeared into the bedroom where the other television is. I turned down the one in the living room; I figured I'd be rid of these two double quick and J.T. could come back out again.

Are you Gracie Mae Still? asked the old guy, when I opened the door and put my hand on the lock inside the screen.

And I don't need to buy a thing, said I.

What makes you think we're sellin'? he asks, in that hearty Southern way that makes my eyeballs ache.

Well, one way or another and they're inside the house and the first thing the young fellow does is raise the TV a couple of decibels. He's about five feet nine, sort of womanish looking, with real dark white skin and a red pouting mouth. His hair is black and curly and he looks like a Loosianna creole.

About one of your songs, says the deacon. He is maybe sixty, with white hair and beard, white silk shirt, black linen suit, black tie and black shoes. His cold gray eyes look like they're sweating.

One of my songs?

Traynor here just *loves* your songs. Don't you, Traynor? He nudges Traynor with his elbow. Traynor blinks, says something I can't catch in a pitch I don't register.

The boy learned to sing and dance livin' round you people out in the country. Practically cut his teeth on you.

Traynor looks up at me and bites his thumbnail.

I laugh.

Well, one way or another they leave with my agreement that they can record one of my songs. The deacon writes me a check for five hundred dollars, the boy grunts his awareness of the transaction, and I am laughing all over myself by the time I rejoin J.T.

Just as I am snuggling down beside him though I hear the front door bell going off again.

Forgit his hat? asks J.T.

I hope not, I say.

The deacon stands there leaning on the door frame and once again I'm thinking of those sweaty-looking eyeballs of his. I wonder if sweat makes your eyeballs pink because his are sure pink. Pink and gray and it strikes me that nobody I'd care to know is behind them.

I forgot one little thing, he says pleasantly. I forgot to tell you Traynor and I would like to buy up all of those records you made of the song. I tell you we sure do love it.

Well, love it or not, I'm not so stupid as to let them do that without making 'em pay. So I says, Well, that's gonna cost you. Because, really, that song never did sell all that good, so I was glad they was going to buy it up.

Elethia

A certain perverse experience shaped Elethia's life, and made it possible for it to be true that she carried with her at all times a small apothecary jar of ashes.

There was in the town where she was born a man whose ancestors had owned a large plantation on which everything under the sun was made or grown. There had been many slaves, and though slavery no longer existed, this grandson of former slaveowners held a quaint proprietary point of view where colored people were concerned. He adored them, of course. Not in the present – it went without saying – but at that time, stopped, just on the outskirts of his memory: his grandfather's time.

This man, whom Elethia never saw, opened a locally famous restaurant on a busy street near the center of town. He called it 'Old Uncle Albert's'. In the window of the restaurant was a stuffed likeness of Uncle Albert himself, a small brown dummy of waxen skin and glittery black eyes. His lips were intensely smiling and his false teeth shone. He carried a covered tray in one hand, raised level with his shoulder, and over his other arm was draped a white napkin.

Black people could not eat at Uncle Albert's, though they worked, of course, in the kitchen. But on Saturday afternoons a crowd of them would gather to look at 'Uncle Albert' and discuss how near to the real person the dummy looked. Only the very old people remembered Albert Porter, and their eyesight was no better than their memory. Still there was a comfort somehow in knowing that Albert's likeness was here before them daily and that if he smiled as a dummy in a fashion he was not known to do as a man, well, perhaps both memory and eyesight were wrong.

The old people appeared grateful to the rich man who owned the restaurant for giving them a taste of vicarious fame.

They could pass by the gleaming window where Uncle Albert stood, seemingly in the act of sprinting forward with his tray, and know that though niggers were not allowed in the front door, ole Albert was already inside, and looking mighty pleased about it, too.

For Elethia the fascination was in Uncle Albert's fingernails. She wondered how his creator had got them on. She wondered also about the white hair that shone so brightly under the lights. One summer she worked as a salad girl in the restaurant's kitchen, and it was she who discovered the truth about Uncle Albert. He was not a dummy; he was stuffed. Like a bird, like a moose's head, like a giant bass. He was stuffed.

One night after the restaurant was closed someone broke in and stole nothing but Uncle Albert. It was Elethia and her friends, boys who were in her class and who called her 'Thia'. Boys who bought Thunderbird and shared it with her. Boys who laughed at her jokes so much they hardly remembered she was also cute. Her tight buddies. They carefully burned Uncle Albert to ashes in the incinerator of their high school, and each of them kept a bottle of his ashes. And for each of them what they knew and their reaction to what they knew was profound.

The experience undercut whatever solid foundation Elethia had assumed she had. She became secretive, wary, looking over her shoulder at the slightest noise. She haunted the museums of any city in which she found herself, looking, usually, at the remains of Indians, for they were plentiful everywhere she went. She discovered some of the Indian warriors and maidens in the museums were also real, stuffed people, painted and wigged and robed, like figures in the Rue Morgue. There were so many, in fact, that she could not possibly steal and burn them all. Besides, she did not know if these figures

41

– with their valiant glass eyes – would wish to be burned.

About Uncle Albert she felt she knew.

What kind of man was Uncle Albert? Well, the old folks said, he wasn't nobody's uncle and wouldn't sit still for nobody to call him that, either.

Why, said another old-timer, I recalls the time they hung a boy's privates on a post at the end of the street where all the black folks shopped, just to scare us all you understand, and Albert Porter was the one took 'em down and buried 'em. Us never did find the rest of the boy though. It was just like always – they would throw you in the river with a big old green log tied to you, and down to the bottom you sunk.

He continued:

Albert was born in slavery and he remembered that his mama and daddy didn't know nothing about slavery'd done ended for near 'bout ten years, the boss man kept them so ignorant of the law, you understand. So he was a mad so-an'-so when he found out. They used to beat him severe trying to make him forget the past and grin and act like a nigger. (Whenever you saw somebody acting like a nigger, Albert said, you could be sure he seriously disremembered his past.) But he never would. Never

would work in the big house as head servant, neither – always broke up stuff. The master at that time was always going around pinching him too. Looks like he hated Albert more than anything – but he never would let him get a job anywhere else. And Albert never would leave home. Too stubborn.

Stubborn, yes. My land, another one said. That's why it do seem strange to see that dummy that sposed to be ole Albert with his mouth open. All them teeth. Hell, all Albert's teeth was knocked out before he was grown.

Elethia went away to college and her friends went into the army because they were poor and that was the way things were. They discovered Uncle Alberts all over the world. Elethia was especially disheartened to find Uncle Alberts in her textbooks, in the newspapers and on t.v.

Everywhere she looked there was an Uncle Albert (and many Aunt Albertas, it goes without saying).

But she had her jar of ashes, the old-timers' memories written down, and her friends who wrote that in the army they were learning skills that would get them through more than a plate glass window. And she was careful that, no matter how compelling the hype, Uncle Alberts, in her own mind, were not permitted to exist.

The Human Element

Harry West's the name, fitter by trade. I'm working for Dawson Whittaker & Sons, one of the biggest engineering firms round Cressley, and lodging with Mrs Baynes, one of the firm's recommended landladies, up on Mafeking Terrace, not far from the Works. It's an interesting job – I like doing things with my hands – and not a bad screw either, what with bonus and a bit of overtime now and again, and taken all round I'm pretty satisfied. The only thing I could grumble about is some of my mates; but they're not a bad lot really. It must be because I'm a big fair bloke and the sort that likes to think a bit before he opens his mouth that gives them the idea I'm good for a laugh now and then. Some of them seem to think it's proper hilarious that I'm happy with my own company and don't need to go out boozing and skirt-chasing every night in the week to enjoy life. And on Monday mornings, sometimes, when they're feeling a bit flat after a weekend on the beer, they'll try to pull my leg about Ma Baynes and that daughter of hers, Thelma. But they get no change out of me. I just let them talk. Keep yourself to yourself and stay happy – that's my motto. I'm not interested in women anyway; I've got better ways of spending my time, not to mention my money.

I've got something better than any girl: nearly human she is. Only she wears chromium plate and black enamel instead of lipstick and nylons. And she's dependable. Look after her properly and she'll never let you down, which I reckon is more than you can say for most women. Every Saturday afternoon I tune her and polish her for the week. There's no better way of spending a Saturday afternoon: just me and the bike, and no complications. All I ask is to be left alone to enjoy it.

Well, it's summer, and a blazing hot Saturday afternoon, and I'm down on my knees in Ma Baynes's backyard with the motor bike on its stand by the wall, when a shadow falls across and I look up and see Thelma standing there.

'Hello, Arry,' she says, and stands there looking at me with them dull, sort of khaki-coloured eyes of hers that never seem to have any expression in them, so you can't tell what's she thinking, or even if she's not thinking at all, which I reckon is usually the case.

'Oh, hello.' And I turn back to the job and give one of the spindle nuts on the front wheel a twist with the spanner.

'Are you busy?' she says then.
I'm trying my best to look that way, hoping she'll take the hint and leave me alone. 'You're allus busy with a motor bike if you look after it properly,' I say. But even me giving it to her short and off-hand like that doesn't make her shove off. Instead she flops down behind me, coming right up close so's she can get

43

her knees on my bit of mat and pressing up against me till I can feel her big bust like a big soft cushion against my shoulder.

'What're you doing now, then?' she says.

'Well,' I say, getting ready to answer a lot of daft questions, 'I'm just checkin' 'at me front wheel's on properly. I don't want that to come loose when I'm on the move, y'know.'

'You must be clever to know all about motor bikes,' she says, and I wonder for a second if she's sucking up to me. But I reckon she's too simple for that.

'Oh, I don't know. You get the hang of 'em when you've had one a bit.'

She gives a bit of a wriggle against my shoulder, sort of massaging me with her bust. She doesn't know what she's doing. She's like a big soft lad and the way she chucks herself about. It'd be enough to give ideas to some blokes I could mention. But not me. It does nothing to me, except make me feel uncomfortable. I'm breaking a new pair of shoes in and I've cramp like needles in my left foot. But I can't move an inch with Thelma there behind me, else we'll both fall over.

She gives another wriggle and then gets up, nearly knocking me into the bike headfirst. And when I've got my balance again I stretch my leg out and move my toes about inside the shoe.

'We was wonderin',' Thelma says, 'if you'd like to lend us your portable radio set. Me mam wants to go on a picnic, but me dad wants to listen to the Test Match.'

Now here's a thing. I've got to go canny here. 'Well, er, I dunno . . .' I get up, steady, wiping my neck with my handkerchief, giving myself time to think of an excuse for saying no. I'm always careful with my belongings.

'Oh, we'd look after it,' Thelma says. 'On'y me dad's that stubborn about his cricket, an' me mam won't go without him.'

I know Old Man Baynes and his sport. It's the one thing Ma Baynes can't override him on.

Thelma can see I'm not happy about the radio and she says, 'Why don't you come with us, then you can look after it yourself? We're goin' to Craddle Woods. It'll be lovely up there today.'

I know it will, and I've already thought of having a ride out that way when I've finished cleaning the bike. But this doesn't suit me at all. I haven't been with the Bayneses long and I've been careful not to get too thick with them. Getting mixed up with people always leads to trouble sooner or later. I always reckon the world would be a sight better place if more folk kept themselves to themselves and minded their own business.

But I see that Thelma has a look on her face like a kid that wants to go to the zoo.

'Well, I'd summat else in mind really,' I say, still trying my best to fob her off. 'I was goin' to clean me bike.'

'Clean it!' she says. 'But it's clean. Look how it shines!'

It on'y looks clean,' I say. 'There's dozens o' mucky places 'at you can't see.'

'Well, it can wait, can't it? You don't want to waste this lovely weather, do you?'

I haven't thought of wasting it, not with the nice little ride all planned. But I'm cornered. That's how it is with people. They pin you down till you can't get out any way. I can see Ma Baynes taking offence if I don't lend them the radio now, and that's the last thing I want. No trouble. I'm all for a quiet life. So I give in.

'Okay, then, I'll come.'

think 1 Which author wrote which story? Try to look for common elements between the stories in order to identify the author. Do this alone, and then compare your choices with a partner and discuss the criteria you used to make your decision. These might be:

- vocabulary used;
- type of characters;
- setting in time;
- setting in place;
- topics discussed;
- the messages put across by the author.

Also look critically at your own choices. Did you assume, for instance, that male/ female writers write in a particular way, or from a particular viewpoint?

2 Write a list of factors which make Alice Walker and Stan Barstow's styles distinctive. Some points might be:

- simple/complex vocabulary;
- the use of a particular accent;
- the sense of a particular area of protest;
- the fondness for a particular setting;
- the treatment of women/men.

a Drawing on the above information, write a detailed description of the style of writing used by either Alice Walker or Stan Barstow. Try to imagine the type of person the writer is.

b Decide which story you like best and read through it again carefully. Now write an extra 300 words to add to that story, which can *either* be inserted into the passage *or* follow on naturally from the end. You will need to pay particular attention to the style of the writer.

c Choose another short story writer and read at least two of their short stories; then write an essay comparing and contrasting their style of writing with *either* Alice Walker *or* Stan Barstow. You might like to begin with a story from this book, and then choose another story by the same author.

45

Causes

Protest songs

There are many reasons why people take up a cause. Within this unit you will be looking at several different causes and people's reactions to them. You will also need to form your own opinions about each one.

Look closely at the following two pop songs, both written on a similar topic. 'Masters of War' was written twenty years before 'Russians'. As you read them through, pick out similarities and differences between the two texts.

Masters of War

Come you masters of war
You that build all the guns
You that build the death planes
You that build the big bombs
You that hide behind walls
You that hide behind desks
I just want you to know
I can see through your masks

You that never done nothin'
But build to destroy
You play with my world
Like it's your little toy
You put a gun in my hand
And you hide from my eyes
And you turn and run farther
When the fast bullets fly

Like Judas of old
You lie and deceive
A world war can be won
You want me to believe
But I see through your eyes
I see through your brain
Like I see through the water
That runs down my drain

You fasten the triggers
For the others to fire
Then you sit back and watch
When the death count gets higher
You hide in your mansion
As young people's blood
Flows out of their bodies
And is buried in the mud

You've thrown the worst fear
That can ever be hurled
Fear to bring children
Into the world
For threatenin' my baby

Unborn and unnamed
You ain't worth the blood
That runs in your veins

How much do I know
To talk out of turn
You might say that I'm young
You might say I'm unlearned
But there's one thing I know
Though I'm younger than you
Even Jesus would never
Forgive what you do

Let me ask you one question
Is your money that good
Will it buy you forgiveness
Do you think that it could
I think you will find
When your death takes its toll
All the money you made
Will never buy back your soul

And I hope that you die
And your death'll come soon
I will follow your casket
In the pale afternoon
And I'll watch while you're lowered
Down to your death bed
And I'll stand o'er you're grave
'Till I'm sure that you're dead

Bob Dylan

46

Russians

In Europe and America, there's a
    growing feeling of hysteria
Conditioned to respond to all the threats
In the rhetorical speeches of the Soviets
Mr Krushchev said we will bury you
I don't subscribe to that point of view
It would be such an ignorant thing to do
If the Russians love their children too

How can I save my little boy from
    Oppenheimer's deadly toy
There is no monopoly of common sense
On either side of the political fence
We share the same biology
Regardless of ideology
Believe me when I say to you
I hope the Russians love their children
    too

There is no historical precedent
To put words in the mouth of the
    president
There's no such thing as a winable war
It's a lie we don't believe anymore
Mr Reagan says we will protect you
I don't subscribe to this point of view
Believe me when I say to you
I hope the Russians love their children
    too

We share the same biology
Regardless of ideology
What might save us me and you
Is that the Russians love their children
    too.

Sting

think

1 Working with a partner, find different ways of describing the following:
  - 'masters of war'
  - 'You might say I'm unlearned'
  - 'a growing feeling of hysteria'
  - 'Oppenheimer's deadly toy'
  - 'historical precedent'
2 What attitude do the two writers have towards war?
3 What do both poems say about children?

choose

a Both writers protest against their own powerlessness in the situation of war. Think of a situation in which you have no power and write your own reactions to this. You can choose any format for your writing (speech, song, creative essay, report).
b Write your own song about East/West relations, or any other subject which you feel is raised in the songs above.

p161 **c** Sum up in about 100 words the 'message' of either one of the songs.

1

War and peace

The following article was written in December 1982, a year after the first peace camp was set up at Greenham Common U.S. Airforce base. The same month saw the first mass demonstration at the base. Thousands of women travelled to Greenham to link arms around the base's nine mile fence. This article charts the progress of the camp, during its first year of existence. Read through the passage carefully, and then answer the questions which follow.

Women at the wire

When 40 women and children set off from Cardiff more than a year ago on a 125-mile march to Greenham Common air-base in Berkshire, all they wanted was a public, televised debate with the Ministry of Defence on Government plans to site 96 cruise missiles there. They didn't get it, so they stayed. One bitter winter, two evictions, and several jail sentences later, women are still camped outside the gates, sheltering under the sheets of polythene stretched over washing lines as the cold weather closes in. They are now forbidden to erect 'structures'; recently Newbury's Conservative Council announced that it was seeking an injunction to move them.

A fortnight ago, 23 women were released from prison after serving a two week sentence for refusing to be bound over to keep the peace. Sixteen of them had invaded a sentry box just inside the main gate in response to a rumour that cruise missiles were already in place; the other seven had stopped new sewage pipes being laid, in preparation for the influx of 1,300 American servicemen arriving, with the missiles next December, by

lying down in front of contractors' vehicles.

These cases made national headlines. Indeed, when 11 of the women were freed from East Sutton Park Prison they walked out straight onto the front pages pictured smiling and defiant. Yet for many months after the camp took root, it was virtually ignored by the media, or at best treated as slightly eccentric. Clearly, something remarkable has been taking place.

It is not easy to define the special quality of Greenham. The camp's inhabitants change almost daily, and so does its atmosphere. Women of all kinds have spent time there – from feminists to Tory ladies, from the mystically inclined to the politically dedicated. By far the majority are ordinary women who have decided that the nuclear threat is too serious for them to leave it unchallenged. They have left jobs, studies and husbands to take part. As their leaflet proclaims: 'For centuries women have watched men go off to war: now women are leaving home for peace.'

Helen John, one of the founders, explains: 'Many women associated with the camp had never taken a strong line on anything in their lives before. Many of us didn't feel we had enough experience or understanding of situations around us to express our opinions. But gradually we gained confidence, and the chain reaction has continued.'

Simone Wilkinson, aged 37, has two children. Until a few months ago, she had never dreamt that she might fall foul of the law; now she has served a jail sentence. While she was pregnant with her second child, she met a Japanese woman related to a Hiroshima survivor. The woman told her that even today, in Hiroshima, people never congratulate a woman on becoming pregnant: they just wait silently for nine months because so many children are still being born deformed.

'That reached something deep within me. When I was carrying my first child, I remember I was told I shouldn't smoke, I should drink milk and I should take vitamins. After the child was born, the health visitor said I should do this and do that; the doctor told me I should take care of my child's life. What they were saying was: "You are responsible for the safe passage of that child's life." I'm just picking up that responsibility – I want a safe passage right through for my children.'

Since its inception, the camp has provided a permanent, visible reminder of the Government's plans. It has also prompted other protests through Britain; last year a dozen peace camps – some women only, others mixed – sprang up outside nuclear installations up and down the country. International visitors have exported the idea to their own countries. Earlier this year, two peace camps were set up in the Netherlands (one has now moved on); another mixed camp has been pitched at Comiso, Sicily, where 112 cruise missiles are due to be stationed.

The 'Women only' nature of the protest is seen as crucial. 'In a verbal exchange with the police, even if there's no violence, in an argument with men police will see potential for aggression,' says Simone. The Greenham women see themselves as using traditional expectations of female behaviour – passivity, politeness, emotional frankness – to map out a new domain of political effectiveness.

Hugo Davenport (Observer)

think

1 Which words and phrases suggest support for the campers?
2 Why was the peace camp first set up?
3 What were Simone's main reasons for joining the camp?
4 Why do the protesters see it as important that the camp is for women only?

choose

a This article writes about the Greenham Common peace camp in a positive light, giving voice to the women and their cause. Generally speaking the media coverage of the protest has not been so favourable, focusing on the local and central government's reaction and on the inconvenience to the military. With reference to the article, and using your own imagination, place yourself in the position of an official whose job it is to 'deal' with complaints from various parties.

p168 ▷

Either write a speech with which to address a gathering, *or* a letter to be sent to a pressure group, explaining how you will tackle the difficulties which have arisen.

p156 ▷

b Do you think the women of Greenham should protest as they do? Write an argumentative essay either defending or arguing against their stand.

p152 ▷

c Imagine you are one of the thousands of women travelling to Greenham to take part in the mass demonstration. Write your own impressions of the day, from your first expectations, to your reflections as you travel home.

d Look at the two photos which accompany the article. Write a set of captions to go with each of the pictures, one of which is favourable, one biased against, and one neutral, towards the women.

The following short story shows a family caught up in war. As you read it through you will need to be conscious of two voices which speak through it.

Alice in Wonderland

Alice put pen to paper.

'My dearest son. Everyone is very happy right now, what with the baby coming. Yes! That's right! The baby's coming! In fact, Dr Wilkins is upstairs dealing with the delivery right now!'

Geoff let himself flop back into the hole. Leaning against its grey walls, he picked up his bayonet, and, with a (sickening) smile of satisfaction, carved yet another notch into the butt of his rifle. He searched the bottom of the grotty abode. Having spotted his paper, his pen wasn't hard to find. Geoff flicked the dirt from the page and refocused his thoughts.

'. . . leave has been postponed again, this time because of some new offensive.'

The soldier paused, and surveyed the horizons of his horrific little world. All clear.

'. . . the Turks are launching just west of us. The CO says it won't effect us . . .'

Geoff stopped again. It was the only way he could get anything done out here. Christ, he couldn't even take a leak in peace. Still, it was true, he couldn't be too careful.

'. . . but Head Office wants us here just in case, so they can't let me go right now.'

Pause.

'. . . Still I should be home for Christmas.'

The doctor leaned over the pregnant woman, to address her mother, who was also leaning over the pregnant woman, in order to address the doctor.

'Mrs Church, madam! I do know how to deliver a baby!'

'I don't doubt it Dr Wilkins, sir. But really . . .'

Both fell silent as Ettie started to cry.

'It's my baby,' she wailed, 'don't I have a say?'

Alice pulled her eyes from the staircase, and turned back to the letter.

Spit it out!

Spit it out!

'. . . Ettie sends her love and says she's sorry that she couldn't write to you herself. It sounds like everything is going just fine up there son. By the time I've finished writing this letter, you'll be a father!'

'. . . Anyway Ettie how are you?'

Pause.

'Has the baby been born yet? Well if not, . . .'

A whistle in the air.

Jesus, they must have spotted him!

On the floor!

On the floor!

An explosion, a shudder. A shower of rubble.

Geoff stayed down, waiting for the second impact. It didn't come. The shell must have fallen short. Landed in no-man's land. Lucky.

'. . . and could you try hanging on until I get home!! I want to be with you!'

'. . . We're all looking forward to seeing you at the end of the month Geoff. It's been such a long time since you were home last.'

'Push! Push! Come on push.'

'You'd have laughed at Mrs Gardener's nipper, the other day. "Mrs Bower" she says to me, "My Daddy's got a fat tummy, is he going to have a baby too?" Well Mrs Gardener went scarlet, seized the poor child, and rushed home on the grounds that her dinner was burning! It was all I could do not to laugh until she was out the front door!'

'Push Ettie, you've got to push!'

'Things have been pretty quiet out here lately, all things considered . . .'

Geoff felt a twinge of guilt at this

undeniable untruth. He looked across at the latest blemish on the landscape.

It was only ten yards away.

He continued to gaze around the edges of his own crater. 'I haven't had any action for 3 days . . .'

Look up. More lies.

'Lucky really, otherwise I'd never have time to write this letter!'

'There's not much left to say son, except that you know we all love you.'

'Anyway Ettie, it's time I put down my pen and had something to eat . . .'

'. . . Bye-bye for now, see you soon! Lots of love, Mother.'

'. . . so I'll be saying goodbye for now. Tell mum I miss her. Lots of love Geoff.'

A cry from upstairs. A baby's cry.

Alice's heart leapt. She stood up with a jerk.

Rubble falling. Behind him. Geoff's heart was in his mouth. In one swift motion, he launched himself to his feet, turning, cradling the weapon.

Alice's thighs hit the edge of the sideboard, sending it rocking.

The cup toppled. Fell. And shattered. Shattered.

Tea seeped into the floorboards.

It didn't matter.

A finger squeezed. A bang, a crack. The bullet was already there for him.

Waiting.

Geoff toppled and fell. His face crimson.

Blood seeped into the grey dust, turning it into pink mud.

Trickling –

Dripping –

Wasting –

Alice rushed back to the sideboard, ignoring the smashed teacup.

'PS' she wrote

'It's a girl!'

The Turk let himself flop back into the hole. Leaning against its grey wall he picked up his bayonet, and with a (sickening) smile of satisfaction, carved yet another notch into the butt of his rifle.

'Must write home,' he thought.

Jason Caffrey

 think

1 Who are the two voices in the story?
2 Describe the events which occur in the two different situations.
3 Pick out the words and phrases which indicate the setting in war and domestic life.
4 Which character do you feel the most sympathy for? Give your reasons.

choose

a The story gains much of its effect through the use of two voices, or narratives, which fit together as Geoff's actions link in with the actions at home. Write your own story with more than one voice or narrative. You could refer to *Late Home* (on page 108) as another example of this technique.

b The story gives a picture of harsh reality, where characters are seen to have pleasant and unpleasant sides to their personality, perhaps through the influence of war. For example as Geoff carves another notch on his rifle butt he is also writing home. Write your own short story which reveals good and bad sides to its characters.

c Compare this view of war to the view seen in the next poem. It is a ballad about the war between Iran and Iraq.

Unsung Heroes Called Fanatics

Ten thousand men would gather there
Each Friday until late
To hear the Imam's fiery tongue
Stir up their blood and hate

'Our faith is like a tree,' he'd say,
'Don't think that I am wrong.
The flowing blood of martyred mess
Will make its boughs grow strong.'

His speeches were hypnotic drugs,
His war was being fought,
His words made men lay down their
   lives,
Without a second thought.

Not only men would listen there,
But often children too,
Young boys of less than seventeen,
For whom the words rang true.

So to the schools the soldiers went,
To see if they could try
To find some boys to volunteer
To come with them to die

And from a school of eighty boys
Baseej weren't hard to find,
And when the trucks left the school gate
Not one was left behind.

So through the desert sands they drove,
Beneath the scorching sun.
Each boy dressed in a uniform,
Each carrying a gun.

Each boy received a plastic key,
And learnt you can't live twice.
But if you're killed, the key'd unlock
The gates of paradise.

Their trainer said, 'This war's Sihad,'
A cold, powerful voice,
'That means it's a holy war,
And so you have no choice.'

Then eighty figures all knelt down
To face the holy city
And each boy prayed as he knelt down
For Allah's peace and pity.

The desert night was quiet,
The morning silent too,
The slaughter when would it commence?
Only the Generals knew.

At last the final order came:
'Tomorrow's the big day,
So clean your weapons, little ones
And for the last time pray.'

Some boys died in the minefields
The others in their trench.
Pathetic torn bodies,
The battle's sickly stench.

All eighty school boys died that day
And eighty eighties more.
Whilst in their bunkers
Priest and despot added to their scores.

That day no positions were seized,
But neither were they lost.
The Generals plan a new campaign,
The mothers count the cost.

Yet on the streets and in the mosques
They'll recruit many more.
Their slogans: If it lasts for twenty years,
We'll fight our holy war.

For five years now the blood has flowed.
No sign that it will stop.
The worst crime of the whole thing is
That both sides fight for God.

Darius Bazergan

think

1 What is it that persuades the school children to fight in the war?
2 What objections does the poet have to the war which is taking place?
3 Select one verse which you find particularly effective, and give reasons for your choice.

choose

a Write an *appreciation* of the poem, saying what you like and dislike about it. Which words and phrases do you find particularly effective? Is the message of the poem clear and do you like its use of the ballad form?
b The writer of this poem has strong opinions on the topic he has chosen to write about: the war between Iran and Iraq. Using the ballad form (four line verses with regular rhyme and rhythm), write about something that you feel strongly about.
c Write a description of the images of war put across in any of the extracts in this section so far. You may wish to compare or contrast different passages. Include your own views on the passage or passages chosen.

2 Strong and weak

Many people take up the cause of animal protection based on their own experiences of animal cruelty, or on research. Read through the following fictitious account of the birth of a calf and then read the argumentative essay *The Abuse of Animals*, which follows it. In each case it is important to try to picture the situation described.

The Birth

She stirred, dreamily aware of the sounds of the farm in the early morning. The cows mooed and shifted their hooves noisily on the cobblestones as they milled about in the yard, waiting to be milked. An iron gate clanged, a chain rattled in its ring, the calves pushed impatiently against the heavy wooden door making the bar that fastened it thud dully in its socket. She heard a distant scrape on the milk-house floor, a bucket clanked, soon the rapid throb of the milking machine would begin. She settled more comfortably into her pillow for a few more moments of sleep.

Then a break in the routine of familiar sounds disturbed her. She heard footsteps racing up the path to the house. There was a shout, an incoherent message. The kitchen door banged against the side of the sink as it was thrown roughly open. She sat up. The footsteps burned up the stairs, her bedroom door flung open.

'Ged up! GED UP. Come on. We gotta pull off a calf.'

There was a fleeting expression of irritation in the young woman's face as she recognised the familiar signs of desperate pre-occupation which, for her father, always accompanied moments of tension. She got up and dressed hastily, pulling on whatever came to hand.

Her face wore an impassive closed-off look. In the kitchen she paused to pull on wellington boots. Her mother was there already, just preparing to follow her husband. The two women exchanged glances, 'He's in a proper state.' Her daughter nodded.

Silently they hurried down the path. There was a sudden roar as an engine burst ferociously into life. 'He's going to use the tractor.'

The younger woman stopped, and looked at her mother, her face suddenly pale. 'I'm not helping then', she said.

Her mother looked at her anxiously, 'He'll make you', she said.

The girl hesitated then turned to go inside.

A frantic shout followed her.

'Where's you going? Come on. Hurry up.' Her father half-sat, half-stood on the massive roaring machine, one great fist clenched on the steering wheel, the other halted in the act of forcing the cold solid iron of the gear stick into reverse. His blazing eyes locked her as she paused undecided beside her mother. His face was vicious, his body taut and coiled. She hesitated a moment longer, then turned once more towards him. With furious dexterity he reversed and then turned sharply towards the gate. Her mother cleared a path through the milking cows. He chafed at the slowness of the operation. He shouted at her over the noise of the tractor, upright on the foot plate his face tense and irritable at the delay.

The two women exchanged grim looks as he yelled, 'Open the gate. Never mind the bleddy cows.' Her mother gave a last shake of her stick at the milling herd and then scurried over to unlatch the gate.

The women avoided each other's eyes now. They followed the tractor into the yard. It was facing the open door of the shed.

The cow stood before them, her back legs splayed apart, her body hunched with the tremendous spasms passing through it. Her great head seemed small, dwarfed by the distended barrel of her belly. Her tail was pushed slightly to one side by the slimey pinkish grey nose and ivory forefeet of the unborn calf. The cow swung her drooping head round to look at them, weary from the hours of unproductive labour. Her breath was loud and shallow and every now and then she let out a long shuddering groan.

The farmer was all tension and frantic haste. He hurriedly attached a rope to the tractor, his thick gnarled fingers fumbling awkwardly as he knotted it tight around the cold angles of the iron drawbar. Then he turned his attention to the other end of the rope. The younger woman took a deep breath as she saw him grappling harshly with the tiny forefeet at the straining distended opening of the cow.

He pushed the loop of rope around the two fore feet tucking it firmly back behind the soft white hooves. He pulled the knot tight and then roughly tugged at it to make sure that it held firm. The cow grunted.

Without looking up, his shoulders still hunched over the rope, he ordered, 'Ged on the tractor'. His breath came in short hard pants of effort as he took the weight of the rope. He was absorbed, obsessed with the task of delivering the calf quickly before it suffocated.

'I never drove this one before', the young woman faltered. She looked pale and apprehensive.

'Ged on the tractor,' he repeated. Her excuse, her vacillation infuriated him. He seemed to her deranged almost as he stared intensely into her face forcing her to obey.

She climbed up. Her hands, her knees were shaking. She put the tractor into reverse. Her foot trembled on the clutch, she held the other rigidly stamped down on the brake.

'Let off the clutch when I say.'

He settled the rope round his huge hard fists. He curved his back and spread his feet apart preparing to take the strain. He began to pull. The cow shifted, trying to find a better balance, as she felt the new weight pulling her back.

The girl on the tractor sat straight, her face grim and anxious. Her knuckles were white with the tension of gripping the unfamiliar steering wheel. As the cow groaned the girl winced, the muscles of her shoulders stiffening under her thin shirt. She looked briefly towards her mother, heaving on the rope with her husband, her lower lip clenched between her teeth, her eyes screwed up.

'Now! Go back.'

The girl's spine was like a rod. Her hands and forearms bulged. Her pale face reddened along the cheekbones making her eyes stare more hugely than before. Her thigh muscles were iron hard against her jeans.

'Go back!' he shouted again. He turned his head towards her, the muscles on his neck stood out, perspiration clung to his forehead, all his strength was concentrated on hauling at the rope.

The girl screwed up her face, her lips pressed tightly together, her eyes almost closed. Slowly, imperceptibly, she began to release the clutch. The sound of the engine changed. Her foot was still clamped down on the brake. Gradually, painstakingly, she let the brake pedal gently upwards. She was holding the great mass of solid throbbing iron steady on the clutch. Her mouth twisted in sympathy for the cow as she let the tractor take the strain against the bulging shape of the emerging calf. The rope held taut and the cow let out a deep despairing moan as her body staggered back. The man pulled with all his strength, his wife added her strength to his. For a split second nothing seemed to happen. Suddenly the calf slipped free and plummetted to the ground. As the tension was released the tractor leaped backwards. The girl stamped both feet onto the pedals. The tractor jerked to a standstill. She put the gear stick to neutral and locked the brake into place; her hands and knees trembled and a desire to weep swept over her.

The cow was bleeding but not damaged, she panted a little as she turned to reach her calf. The farmer knelt beside the still form on the floor. It lay wet and unmoving in the straw, its eyes and nose blocked with mucus. With the palm of his hand he wiped away the slime. The head was swollen from the protracted birth. There was no sign of life. Impatiently the man punched the calf in the ribs. The blow made it gasp. It struggled feebly to rise.

Holding it by the head and tail, the farmer dragged it roughly up to the cow's head and let it drop beside her. He unchained the cow and with a soft lowing she began to lick the calf clean. The farmer straightened up. He looked triumphantly towards the two women.

'Twould 'ave been a thousand pound down the drain if we'd lost 'er', he said with deep satisfaction in his voice.

'I'll go and put the kettle on', said his wife.

Jennifer Gubb

The Abuse of Animals

Many people in the so-called civilised western world are by no means happy about the conditions under which our food is produced. Factory farming proves to be a very profitable business which offers more freedom, less responsibility and a much shorter working week. In Britain, a farmer can do as much as he pleases with his animals, and the police and RSPCA inspectors cannot be in every field or barn to watch what he does with his own property. . . Factory farming enables just one person to look after ten thousand hens in a battery house which is fully automatic. Food is measured, each bird getting just the correct amount, the eggs are clean, uniform and unbroken. There is some wastage among birds, which have become virtually egg-laying machines, but the production numbers are so enormous and the turnover so fast that a certain percentage of birds are expendable. In order to turn hens into even more efficient laying-machines, wings are cut to save space in the battery system cages, and beaks are cut to avoid feather picking and cannibalism (brought on by boredom and immobility).

Pigs are kept in similar disgusting, inhuman conditions. One person can feed, water and clean out hundreds of pigs, which in old-type houses with outside runs would be impossible. The pigs convert their food to pork or bacon at an economic ratio. The food conversion can be controlled, and the pig can be graded at just the desired weight required by the market. The pigs know no change of atmosphere and at birth are liable to iron deficiency. It is cruel to keep pigs in a temperature of eighty degrees and to limit their movements. A pig born into a factory farm can never experience the freedom to roam about, no, this luxury is impossible because pigs are practically immobilised from birth to the bacon factory. Some American farmers, however, do not even wait for the moment of birth, because hysterectomy is now widely practiced in the United States of America. The whole uterus is removed from the sow with piglets inside it, and they are then kept in sterile incubators to form the basis of disease-free herds, perfect for human consumption.

It could be said that the worst aspect of battery farming lies in some of the production of battery veal. Calves are taken from their mothers at birth and are then immobilised either by tethering or by being put into crates. The aim is to keep them anaemic so that the whitest possible meat can be produced. The calves are unable to groom themselves and are kept on slatted floors which are extremely uncomfortable for cloven-hoofed animals and result in deformed and swollen joints. These calves are given a maximum of fifteen weeks to live. After this the extreme anaemia introduced by the way of living and diet would cause death in any case, if they were not slaughtered first. Antibiotics as an aid to growth and to prevent an early death are also frequently employed.

Those who defend these inhuman methods point out that the animals are quite happy – they eat well, and either lay well or put on weight, and this is supposed to be an indication of the lack of cruelty. Unhappy animals, it is argued, would not respond in these ways. I do not think that this is a conclusive argument at all. In my opinion it is a pathetic attempt to justify cruelty.

Tanya Nyari

think

1 Pick out those words and phrases in *The Birth* which suggest:
- a romantic view of the farm;
- the cruelty of the farm.

Explain your choices.

2 In what ways is the use of the tractor the most sensible way to help the cow give birth?

choose

p161 ▷ **a** Tanya Nyari and Jennifer Gubb write from a *biased* viewpoint. They have their own opinions on farming, and argue their case persuasively in order to alter the reader's viewpoint. Select the *factual* evidence about factory farming or the rearing of calves and rewrite the information as an *impartial* and *informative* summary.

p156 ▷ **b** Reference is made in the story and the essay to the views of the farmers involved in the farming, but they are not really given a proper platform for debate. Imagine you are a farmer currently involved in battery farming and/or in rearing calves, and write a letter to Tanya Nyari and/or Jennifer Gubb putting forward your case.

p168 ▷ **c** Think of another area in which animals are exploited by humans (the fur trade, experimentation) and carry out some research into the living conditions of the animals in such circumstances. Your local library may help, or the RSPCA. Present your findings in an oral presentation to the class.

d How might the police or RSPCA better enforce controls over the treatment of animals? Write a clear plan, which could be implemented in one county, to ensure that animals were treated fairly.

e Design a leaflet or poster which:
- opposes animal experimentation;
- defends animal experimentation.

Milkman and Guitar have been friends from childhood, but as they have grown older they have developed as very different people. In this extract Milkman asks Guitar to tell him why he has been so secretive recently, and the answer Guitar gives, shows just how different they've become. The novel is set in the southern states of America in the 1950s.

Song of Solomon

Guitar poured some more hot water over his tea. He looked into his cup for a minute while the leaves settled slowly to the bottom. 'I suppose you know that white people kill black people from time to time, and most folks shake their heads and say, "Eh, eh, eh, ain't that a shame?" '

Milkman raised his eyebrows. He thought Guitar was going to let him in on some deal he had going. But he was slipping into his race bag. He was speaking slowly, as though each word had to count, and as though he were listening carefully to his own words. 'I can't suck my teeth or say "Eh, eh, eh." I had to do something. And the only thing left to do is balance it; keep things on an even keel. Any man, any woman, or any child is good for five or seven generations of heirs before they're bred out. So every death is the death of five to seven generations. You can't stop them from killing us, from trying to get rid of us. And each time they succeed, they get rid of five to seven generations. I help keep the numbers the same.'

'There is a society. It's made up of a few men who are willing to take some risks. They don't initiate anything; they don't even choose. They are as indifferent as rain. But when a Negro child, Negro woman, or Negro man is killed by whites and nothing is done about it in *their* courts, this society selects a similar victim at random, and they execute him or her in a similar manner if they can. If the Negro was hanged, they hang; if a Negro was burnt, they burn; raped and murdered they rape and murder. If they can. If they can't do it precisely in the same manner, they do it any way they can, but they do it. They call themselves the Seven Days. They are made up of seven men. Always seven and only seven. If one of them dies or leaves or is no longer effective, another is chosen. Not right away, because that kind of choosing takes time. But they don't seem to be in a hurry. Their secret is time. To take the time, to last. Not to grow; that's dangerous because you might become known. They don't write their names on toilet stalls, or brag to women. Time and silence. Those are their weapons and they go on for ever.'

'It got started in 1920, when that private from Georgia was killed after his balls were cut off and after that veteran was blinded when he came home from France in World War 1. And it's been operating ever since. I am one of them now.'

Milkman held himself very still all the time Guitar spoke. Now he felt tight, shrivelled and cold.

'You? You're going to kill people?'

'Not people. White people.'

'But why?'

'I just told you. It's necessary; it's got to be done. To keep the ratio the same.'

'And if it isn't done? If it just goes on the way it has?

'Then the world is a zoo, and I can't live in it.'

'Why don't you just hunt down the ones who did the killing? Why kill innocent people? Why not just the ones who did it?'

'It doesn't matter who did it. Each and every one of them could do it. So you just get any one of them. There are no innocent white people, because every one of them is a potential nigger-killer, if not an actual one. You think Hitler surprised them? You think just because they went to war they thought he was a freak? Hitler's the most natural white man in the world. He killed Jews and Gypsies because he didn't have us. Can you see those Klansmen shocked by him? No, you can't.'

'But people who lynch and slice off people's balls – they're crazy Guitar, crazy.'

Every time somebody does a thing like that to one of us, they say the people who did it were crazy or ignorant. That's like saying they were drunk. Or constipated. Why isn't cutting a man's eyes out, cutting his nuts off, the kind of thing you never get too drunk or too ignorant to do? Too crazy to do? Too constipated to do? And more to the point, how come Negroes, the craziest, most ignorant people in America, don't get that crazy and that ignorant? No. White people are unnatural. As a race they are unnatural. And it takes a strong effort of the will to overcome an unnatural enemy.'

Toni Morrison

think

1 What is the secret that Guitar tells Milkman?
2 What are Milkman's reactions to what he is told?
3 In what way are the white people 'unnatural'?
4 Do you think that in the situation described Guitar's actions are justifiable?

choose

p156 ▷

a Imagine you are Milkman and that your best friend has just told you he is one of seven people who aim to kill white people. What would you do? Write a letter to Guitar describing the course of action you intend to take, and giving your reasons. Remember you are writing to a friend.

p174 ▷

b One of the other members of the society finds out that Guitar has told someone about the society. He informs the other members and they decide to meet to discuss what to do, without Guitar present! Act out the meeting in a piece of role play which can be taped or shown to the rest of the group.

p161 ▷

c Guitar acts because when black people were murdered at this time nothing was done about it. What could have been done *within* the law? Write a report suggesting various ways in which the white killers could be brought to justice.

Charities are, by definition, organizations set up to further someone's cause for them, because they are unable to do so themselves.

Look closely at the advertisements which follow. Both are asking you to sponsor a child in a developing country. Charities are gradually altering their approach to advertising in response to a change in their work. Whereas previously Europeans were sent to developing countries as care workers (e.g. doctors and nurses), they are increasingly going as advisors to native care staff (to train doctors and nurses from inside the community). The argument behind this is that a country should be helped to make money from its own resources and train its own people rather than being pushed into taking money and experts from other countries.

Thus advertising is moving from portraits of weak and helpless victims, to images of people with a potential for strength, who are in need of financial assistance. It remains to be seen whether the new approach will raise funds as successfully as the old.

think

1 Which advert suggests from its main picture that children are 'victims' needing to be looked after by 'you'?

2 Which advert shows the child as strong but in need of financial help?

3 Which advert do you find the most striking? Why?

4 Pick out the words, phrases and images in the advertisements which are emotive, and demand an emotional response from the reader.

choose

a Compare and contrast the advertisements shown. Decide, in each case, what message is being put across in terms of:
  - the help needed;
  - the character of those who need help.

b Design your own advertisement to encourage someone to give money to sponsor a child. You don't have to follow the pattern of the ones above; your only guideline is that the advertisement must encourage people to give money.

c What are your reactions to giving money to the Third World? Do you think it should be encouraged; taken on by governments; or banned as it plays on people's guilt and gives a negative image of developing countries? Write an essay explaining your own viewpoint.

p152 **d** 'Charity dignifies the giver. Charity takes dignity away from the receiver.' Write your response to this statement as an argumentative essay, or a creative piece.

Why your giving should be directed to **Crisis Prevention** and to the small lives who are the hope and the future of Third World communities on the edge of survival.

When disaster strikes, the children are the weakest point. They die in their hundreds of thousands from famine and turbulence made by men or by nature.

World Vision responds to these heartbreaking calamities, directing the giving of countless generous donors to where the need is. Yet we, like them, ask the inevitable question: can't we prevent this pain?

Our response is to redouble efforts to prompt self-reliance in communities who want a hand up, not a hand-out. Whether in city slums or failing rural villages, there are opportunities to fight poverty, to prevent crises.

We work through children to their families and their people, believing that they are the future. Our approach is one-at-a-time, looking for the communities themselves to find their own direction, supporting them with sponsorship and other funds, only bringing in the skills they don't have.

World Vision notes that the sort of major Third World social reform designed to 'filter down' seldom reaches the poor and the powerless. Instead, their deprivation usually increases.

Our part is to encourage change, starting from their level, **upwards**. This is the quiet, caring, determined work of Crisis Prevention, working with one person – one child at a time.

If you agree with this approach, join us as a sponsor or donor, now.

WORLD VISION
Practical Christian Caring

Dychurch House, Abington Street, Northampton, NN1 2AJ. Tel. Northampton (0604) 22964
Registered Charity no. 285908

 **Personal causes**

Maya Angelou was born in St. Louis, Missouri, in 1928. She has written five volumes of autobiography, which tell of her struggles as a black woman in America. The following poem gives insight into her own experiences of prejudice as a black woman. As you read through the poem, try to imagine what emotions she may have experienced in writing the piece.

Still I Rise

You may write me down in history
With your bitter twisted lies
You may trod me in the very dirt
But still, like dust I rise.

Does my sassiness upset you?
Why are you beset with gloom?
'Cause I walk like I've got oil wells
Pumping in my living room.

Just like moons and like suns
With the certainty of tides
Just like hopes springing high
Still I rise.

Did you want to see me broken?
Bowed head and lowered eyes?
Shoulders falling down like teardrops
Weakened by my soulful cries.

Does my haughtiness offend you?
Don't you take it awful hard
'Cause I laugh like I've got gold mines
Diggin' in my own back yard.

You may shoot me with your words,
You may cut me with your eyes,
You may kill me with your hatefulness,
But still, like air, I'll rise.

Does my sexiness upset you?
Does it come as a surprise
That I dance like I've got diamonds
At the meeting of my thighs.

Out of the huts of history's shame
I rise
Up from a past that's rooted in pain
I rise
I'm a black ocean, leaping and wide,
Welling and swelling I bear in the tide.

Leaving behind nights of terror and fear
I rise
Into a daybreak that's wondrously clear
I rise
Bringing the gifts that my ancestors
    gave,
I am the dream and the hope of the slave.
I rise
I rise
I rise.

Maya Angelou

think
1   Who do you think the 'you' is in the poem?
2   What do you think is meant by the first two lines of the poem? (Looking at verse 8 may give you some ideas.)
3   In what ways do you think the poet will 'rise'?

choose
p156 ▷

a   If Maya Angelou had not written these ideas in a poem, she might have decided to address the 'you' character in another form, perhaps a letter of complaint. Write the formal letter which you think she might have written, trying to express as many as possible of the complaints that she mentions in the poem.
b   Much of Maya Angelou's anger is directed towards the misrepresentation of black people in History and Geography text books, which are supposed to give 'facts'

which are, by definition, the 'truth'. Carry out some research into the History or Georgraphy books in your school or local library. Are there any instances where black people are shown unfairly or untruthfully? Keep detailed notes throughout your research and report your findings to the group.

p163 c As an extended project, read one of Maya Angelou's biographies. Write a review of the book as an informative piece of writing. The books are titled:

I Know Why the Caged Bird Sings
Gather Together in my Name
Singin' and Swingin'
The Heart of a Woman
Just Give Me a Cool Drink of Water

The Media

My Life Gazette

How often have you read the paper or listened to the TV news and thought: 'this has nothing to do with me, it is not my experience of the world'? Yet we often gain our world picture from the media rather than from our own experience. We rely on the information the media gives us, to find out about places we have never seen.

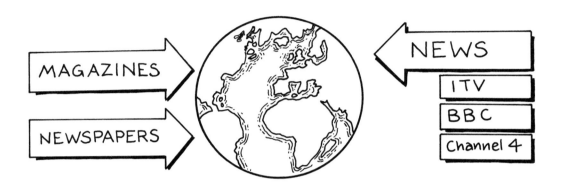

What would the news headlines be like if you based them purely on your own experiences?

BONG	Youth kept up all night by screaming baby brother.
BONG	Major tests to be carried out in Geography.
BONG	Pocket money at all time low.
BONG	Another spot erupts, experience says more will follow.
BONG	Still no luck in finding a partner for the dance competition.

Write your own headlines for today and then write an article to accompany one of them. Make sure you think about the sort of language the media uses. For example:

ANOTHER SPOT ERUPTS, EXPERIENCE SAYS MANY MORE WILL FOLLOW.

Reports came in early this morning of another spot sighting in Peckham. The witness said: 'I looked in the mirror and there it was, it was horrible, a nightmare.'

'Do you know anything which may have caused this eruption?'

'Well, I feel it may be related to a non-washing situation which came upon me last night, after watching the late film, and then of course there is the fry-up I had at lunchtime.'

'So there you have it, will the problem increase? We'll have to wait and see. A cautionary tale about the dangers of late night films!'

Of course these ideas are not serious. Below is a rather more serious profile of a person's day.

I start my day the Valium way at 7.20am when my departing husband brings me a mug of tea and a diazepan tablet. A Valium a day keeps psychiatrists at bay . . .

I loathe, I hate, I abhor housework. Nevertheless, that's what I do next. Only trendy, middle-class lady journalists like Jilly Cooper can get away with having mucky houses. Not that they want to; quite the reverse, in fact. Have you noticed how it's a compulsion with them to boast about how the cat was sick in the *boeuf bourguignon*? Or how they failed to notice that the stripped pine dresser – picked up in a junk shop for £15 – was feet thick in dust until friends wrote rude words on it with damp index fingers?

Down here in working-class land you'd be excommunicated for far less than that. Among us lower orders cleanliness isn't next to godliness: they are one and the same thing.

Diane Harpwood

1 Is it reality?

On page 69 you will find the front pages of three papers all published on the same day, Monday 23rd February 1987. The tables below show the main headline in each paper, the main picture, and the items which were covered on the front page.

Spend some time examining this information and then answer the questions on the next page.

Main Headlines
The Times: June Summit Threatened by 'snub' to Italy
Today: Trapped by a Hamster
The Independent: Tory MPs threaten to leave Church

Main Pictures
The Times: Syrian tanks
Today: Princess Diana
The Independent: Word champion boxing

Front page articles

	Times	Today	Independent
Syrian troops moving into Beirut	*		*
Women as Anglican Clergy			*
Actione Directe members arrested		*	*
Deal to stabalize the dollar			*
Death of Andy Warhol	*		*
Manufacturing at high levels	*		*
Judge's wife sent poison sweets			*
Summit threatened by snub to Italy	*		
Iran situation worsens	*		
More money to space research	*		
New Westland dispute	*		
Labour's non-nuclear stand	*		
Boxing champioinship – Honeyghan	*	*	*
Diana flies home alone		*	

1 Which story do all the papers report on their front page?

2 Comment on the different style of headlines and sub-headings used by the different papers.

3 Here are four different headlines for the same story:
- 'Key terror suspects detained'
- 'Trapped by a hamster'
- 'French seize four left-wing extremists'
- 'Leaders of Actione Directe terrorist group seized'

What differences in attitude are implied in each headline? Who does each headline appeal to?

a Every newspaper is written to be read by a particular audience. Journalists and editors have to angle their news in order to please their readership, and so ensure that they keep reading their paper. Look at the papers above and decide which of the following people would be likely to buy each paper.

Mrs Right works in the Stock Exchange and her husband is a banker. She voted Conservative in the last election. She has a degree in Finance and has always been interested in world politics. She commutes to London, and so has plenty of reading time.

Ms Jackson is an office clerk in an Estate Agents. She likes to do a fairly simple crossword, enjoys following the sports news, and likes a paper to be entertaining rather than too serious.

Mr Rees is a teacher. He likes to follow current affairs, but doesn't have much time to read the paper. He also wants to know what's on the television.

Mr Harding is a carpenter. He doesn't enjoy reading but wants to know what's going on in the world. He likes the 'human interest' stories best, rather than learning about government reports. He also likes to read his horoscope.

Now create some profiles of your own, and decide which paper they would be most likely to read.

p161   **b**   Write a report to summarize the information given on the previous pages. Make it as interesting as possible, but try to avoid giving *your* views on the information.

   c   Prepare a talk for the class, highlighting the different ways in which newspapers
p175   present their stories. You will need to consider the balance of pictures and printing, the size and phraseology of the headlines, and the choice of front page stories. You will also need to look at the balance of stories on:

- human interest;
- politics;
- world affairs.

Satire on the media is common. Sometimes it takes the form of a gentle ridicule, and at other times a serious attack. Read through the following poem by Steve Turner and decide what it is the writer is criticizing. Pick out the words and phrases which indicate how strongly he feels about the criticism he is making.

Exclusive Pictures

Give us good pictures
of the human torch
which show the skin
burnt like chicken,
bursting like grapes.

It will teach us
to avoid flames.

Give us good film
of the lady on the ledge
as she leaps open mouthed
and hits the streets
like a suicide.

It will teach us
to use stairways.

Give us sharp colour
coverage of the African
troubles. Show us
interesting wounds,
craters in fat and flesh.

It will teach us
not to point guns.

Give us five page spreads
of the airliner that fell
like a pigeon to the ground.
And make sure you get there
before the victims are pulled out.

It will teach
engines to function.

Don't give us
any of that shaky
hand-held stuff
where the trapped children
are smoke-like shapes
and their screams barely audible
beneath the wailing sirens.

Get in there with your lenses
and your appetite for danger
and your hard news head
and give us what we're after.
Make us informed.
Make us feel we're really there.
Provide us with education.
Broaden our backgrounds.
We live in a democracy
and we need to know.

Steve Turner

 **a** Write your own poem about one aspect of the media you disapprove of.
b Steve Turner gets much of the impact of the poem 'Exclusive Pictures' from the use of:

- repetition;
- commands (which might come from a news editor);
- common knowledge situations (the person on the window ledge commiting suicide/a plane crash);
- unpleasant images pushed towards us, just as the pictures themselves would be.

Write your own poem on another subject, which uses some or all of the same techniques.

c What might Steve Turner have written if he had chosen to write in a format other than poetry? Write the ideas expressed in the poem using one of the following formats:

- a letter to a newspaper;
- an argumentative essay;
- a short story;
- a radio play;
- a party political broadcast.

The following passage is taken from an article written in response to an S.A.S. procedure which ended a terrorist seige. The writer shows throughout the piece that he saw the event as over-glamourized by the press. Read through the passage carefully and answer the questions which follow.

It had all the ingredients. More than all. In showbiz terms it was over the top. A Bank Holiday, so everyone was home for the first live political siege to be televised on British soil. For an audience, take a sensitive, deeply patriotic nation deprived of the fun of war and the status of a Great Power, still bogged down in TV soap opera of how it licked the Germans and tamed the colonial native, and increasingly wedded to such hazardous leisure substitutes as pot-holing, car-racing, hang-gliding, singlehanded sailing, cliff climbing, ambulance strikes and football aggro.

A hit-team of black-uniformed frogmen is roping down the side of an embassy, Action-Man personified, stepping off the back of our cereal packets and performing the impossible, Britain's own Dirty Dozen. Before our very eyes the sleeping psychopath in all of us was called to arms, institutionalised, dressed in black and licensed to kill. A bunch of 007s on a tight rein, their violent appetites canalised to the public good, *live on screen* at peak viewing time; and best of all, British.

A John Wayne Western on BBC1 had to be interrupted: Wayne the gun-lover, the rightwing crusader, the lone believer in death to the wets and victory to the brave, was for once out-gunned. My seven-year-old son was indignant. After a couple of minutes of the real thing, he found the reality formless and wanted to go back to Wayne and clearer issues. His feelings, as we now know from the BBC, were shared by a great many adult viewers who phoned in to complain. And by a Mr Chambers from Keele who wrote to the *Guardian* to complain that the Beeb had ruined his TV snooker on BBC2.

In those intense few minutes we, the public, were mini-hostages. Ignorant of practically everything that was going on before our eyes, unable in our millions to influence the outcome by a brush stroke, we passed through a miniaturised syndrome of anxiety, dismay, perplexity, dependence and rejection, which turned our drawing-rooms into flight-simulators of the live disaster we believed that we were witnessing. And when the impossible happened, and the tragedy became a triumph, we emerged from the imprisonment of that hateful little screen and, thus conditioned, embraced Authority as our saviour.

Our policemen were wonderful after all. PC Dixon of Dock Green, far from dead, walked and talked in the even less perturbable shape of his splendid familiar, PC Lock. Our shock troops were best, *the best in the world*, and we ourselves, by extension, were to be congratulated – our leaders told it to us in so many words, though they told us precious little else – for having engendered these sons of Britain.

The siege of Princes Gate – it was quickly made clear by Press and Parliament – showed what Britain could do when she wasn't being wet – and God help the man, myself included, who goads the British when they are in this mood; least of all after they have been so effectively manipulated by the Box. We knew nothing then, and if the authorities had their way, we would know precious little now. But it is axiomatic of this type of operation that the collective should have no part in it and the public should be proud of its ignorance.

On the morning following the siege I took an early walk on Hampstead Heath. Sometimes at that time of day, you see a pale blue police car patrolling one of the tarmac paths at a stately five miles an hour. Perhaps it was only my imagination, but on that day the police car seemed to be travelling a great deal faster, and with a lot less concern for the public it was there to protect.

I grabbed my son's dog and tried to wish them good morning at the same time, because the patriot in me, or the citizen, really wanted to show a human face, and see one in return. They shot past me and all I saw was four hostile eyes looking me up and down. Perhaps they were tired. Perhaps they were hunting for a rapist. But I still wish they'd smiled. Do you know that feeling these days? I seem to get it more and more.

John Le Carré

think

1 With which programmes does Le Carré compare the siege coverage?
2 How was the siege covered by the press?
3 Apart from the media coverage, what else does Le Carré object to in the siege?
4 What point is being made in the final paragraphs?
5 Work with a partner to discuss your views on relationships between the police and the public today.

choose

a Le Carré's style of writing manages to capture the excitement of a John Wayne movie whilst expressing disapproval at what is going on. Look closely at the *style* of his writing and then try to imitate it, using a subject of your own choice to write on. Things you should consider are:
   - the length of the sentences;
   - the use of italics;
   - the mocking tone;
   - comparing reality with television fiction.

b Using any news item currently being reported, discuss how reporters may be glamourizing news stories, to ensure that their audience is kept interested. Rewrite any current news item in:
   - a more 'glamorous' way;
   - a less 'dramatic' way.

The following article, taken from the *Sunday Observer*, looks at the way in which the ITN News is put together. It also shows the variation in news covered by ITV and BBC on the same day. Read through the passage carefully and then complete the assignments which follow.

Biased, trivial, showbizzy, self-satisfied, inaccurate, distorted . . . nearly every pejorative adjective, as well as many congratulatory ones, has been applied to television news, the source, so it is said, of most people's idea of what is happening in the world on any given day.

ITN and BBC tread a difficult path between entertainment and journalism. Their formulas are similar: two people reading alternate snippets short enough for the most limited attention span, lots of pictures and diagrams, and a knowing smirk after the final 'soft' item – frequently about animals or royalty – designed to send viewers away with a chuckle and the feeling that the world is not such a bad place after all. There are the occasional squirm-inducing questions – 'How do you feel now that your son has been shot/daughter raped/husband killed in a car crash' – and a general feeling that news values are based on pictures that support the prejudices of urban, middle-class males. Both organisations respect each other, but both can produce statistics to illustrate their own superiority.

ITN's 'News at Ten'
'News at Ten', Friday 12 December
Audience: 7.2 million (source: BARB)
Newscasters: Sandy Gall and Carol Barnes
Annual budget: £50 million (for all news programmes, including 'Channel Four News'). Total for three main daily bulletins plus weekend bulletins on ITV: £37 million
Staff: 950 (total news staff)
The ITN newsroom on the sixth floor of a cramped office in Wells Street has the dingy feel of an old-fashioned newspaper office. The company is looking for new premises.

'We've got a pretty good menu today, though. It's the eternal trade-off – with all this good stuff coming in, do you cut it fairly tight and run a long bulletin with minute and a halfers, or do you, as I prefer, go a bundle on two or three and get the others down very tight? The ideal news is one where there isn't much left for the morning papers.

'The criticism I find hardest to face is that television news is oriented too much to the male. All the time one is trying to find something to say in the "bongs" [headlines] that is going to keep the mum interested – consumer stories and the Royal Family. I don't think there's too much on the Royal Family. In a melancholy world a newscast can go beyond the threshold of pain and so we're always on the look-out for something upbeat as a counterpoint.'

Sir Alastair Burnet declined to answer questions about 'In Private, In Public'*, but Nicholas said, 'The public loved it, even if newspapers hated it. I cannot see that it was obsequious. All the tough, pop questions were there – "Is it true you quarrel like hell with Princess Anne?" "Are you anorexic?" But because Alastair doesn't hector and shout, it's translated differently.'

By the time of the 3pm meeting in Burnet's office, senior editor Sue Tinson is well pleased with the day's potential. 'We've a lot of good visual packages and non in-house stories. Because there's so much around we're going to have to be ruthless and I'm cutting down on the rape case,' she says. 'I've left the Queen in because there are nice pictures of her going round Sheffield Wednesday football ground. *Today* is sending us their front page because they claim Myra Hindley is going to the Moors next week . . .'

*A programme about Prince Charles and Princess Diana.

There is some scepticism. 'They're using us,' says Nicholas. 'Besides, they said that Princess Anne was pregnant.' He suggests trying to get a comment from Detective Chief Superintendent Peter Topping based on the front page story. 'Shouldn't we talk to the parents who are trying to kill her?' asks Carol Barnes.

It is decided to start part two with the first colour pictures inside the Duke and Duchess of Windsor's house, and follow with the weekly job survey, which many think is rather meaningless. 'We couldn't drop it because that would be too much of a political statement,' says Sue Tinson. 'It would imply the end of unemployment.'

The BBC six o'clock news again leads with South Africa. 'That story hasn't moved much,' says Tinson, who still plans to lead with the Khashoggi interview, which is not even mentioned on the BBC. 'In their case I would do the same. I've led on something different when I know the BBC have better pictures.'

Neil Kinnock, interviewed on Channel 4's 'A Week in Politics', has said Labour would remove nuclear weapons within one Parliament. 'It's the usual old fudge, I'm afraid,' says Tinson. 'But we also have Shultz slagging him off at the NATO conference. For the last story, it's a toss-up between the America's Cup and an old folks' party in prison. The America's Cup is sad so, as it's Friday, let's end on the prison.'

At eight o'clock there is a shipwreck off the Isles of Scilly, news comes of Reagan asking his aides to testify truthfully, and film of the old people's party is hazy. 'There was a time when, for three months, every interview with Tony Benn went wrong for technical reasons, but he didn't believe in the cock-up

73

theory of things,' says Tinson. At 9.40 there is a report of a plane crash in East Germany – 'Could be rather nasty,' says Tinson – and another ship is in trouble. Reporters are assigned to the stories. A few minutes before transmission, the 'bongs' are recorded by Sandy Gall; half an hour later, for better or worse, millions of people have had their final fix on what happened during the day.

BBC's 'Nine O'Clock News'
Items on 12 December 1986

1 South Africa.
2 Inquiry into loss of freighter Derbyshire.
3 Doctor cleared of rape. Long filmed report.
4 CIA official challenges Peter Wright's book.
5 Straightforward report of NATO foreign ministers' meeting.
6 President Reagan says he won't be undermined by Iran arms scandal.
7 Soviet airline crash.
8 Inflation up.
9 British Gas sale revenue.
10 British Telecom announce lay-offs.
11 Teachers' Union accepts pay offer.
12 The Queen at Cortonwood.
13 Long report on Blyth Valley MP John Ryman threatening to resign.
14 Straight report of dairy worker killed in explosion at County Tyrone.
15 Fashion designers say it is the worst year for theft.
16 Second Test Match report.
17 One soccer result.
18 Las Vegas slot machine pay-out of $2.5 million.

ITN's 'News at Ten'
Items on 12 December 1986

1 President Reagan reported to have told aides 'Tell all you know' to the Congressional investigators. ABC film of Khashoggi interview.
2 South Africa.
3 Kinnock says Labour Government would remove nuclear weapons within one Parliament.
4 Russian airliner crash.
5 Cargo ship drifts out of control towards Scillies.
6 Doctor cleared of rape. Short item.
7 Dairy worker killed in County Tyrone, followed by long report on MI5 involvement in Ireland.
8 Peter Wright describes Margaret Thatcher as 'stubborn'. First look at the manuscript of his book.
9 Duchess of Windsor's Paris home.
10 Psychological problems of train drivers who hit suicides.
11 Inflation up.
12 British Telecom.
13 Job survey.
14 Inquiry into the Derbyshire.
15 One soccer result.
16 Test Match.
17 America's Cup row.
18 Prison party for OAPs.

think

1 Why do you think the writer describes the newsroom so clearly?
2 Why is the news described as people's 'daily fix'?
3 Which aspects of a story make it 'good' news so that it is worth showing?

choose

a Of the eighteen items mentioned on the ITN news, how many are seen as of the same importance by both channels? Imagine you are a news editor who has to justify the news which went out on 12 December. Write a letter to your superior explaining why you chose the items you did.

p156 ▷

b Write a news reporter's diary for a day, gleaning your information from the passage above. Which parts of the day do you find the most rewarding or frustrating? Why did you choose this job?

p159 ▷

c Watch or listen to different TV or radio news bulletins on one day. To what extent do they differ? Which news coverage did you find the most satisfactory?

2

Images

Look carefully at the extracts below which are taken from various girl's magazines.

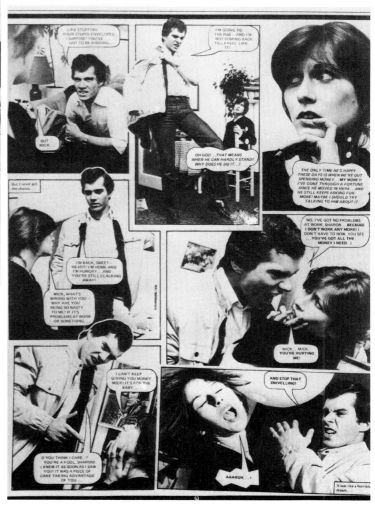

think **1** Which of the following images can you find in them?

2 Which other character traits did you notice as being 'typical' of boys and girls, and men and women?

3 Here is one way of breaking down the images to see how they are created. *GLAMOUR*:

- lifestyle;
- physical appearance (long blond/red hair, 'no-blemish' face, hour-glass figure);
- words.

Select any two of the traits seen in the magazine and break them down, as with the one above.

choose **a** Comic strips are also powerful ways of telling a story, as they link the visual and written form. Decide which of the above stories you find the least and most appealing, and state what it is about them you like/dislike. Think about:

- the use of pictures shot close up and at a distance;
- the overall page design;
- the use of 'bubble speech' and story line boxes;
- the passage of time as shown in the stories;
- the use of photos versus the use of an artist's drawing;
- the language used by the male and female characters;
- storyline boxes.

Rewrite the cartoon story you like best, as a prose story.

b Create a storyline which does not allow men and women to act in the stereotyped ways seen above. You might decide, for instance, to have men who are allowed to cry, and women who are allowed to make decisions. You can choose a story or cartoon format.

c What were your favourite comics when you were younger? How far do you think they have affected your views or lifestyle? First spend some time thinking and then organize a small group discussion on this subject.

d Do you think these magazines simply reflect the views we already have of men and women, or do they brainwash us into holding certain views? Interview some of the people in your class to get their ideas on this question and then write up your findings.

e The following love sonnet uses typical images of women but to a humorous end.

Italian Beauty

You are the most lovely, I do not lie.
For men everywhere you're a sight to see.
Your body's well shaped, it pleases the eye.
Your youth's eternal, you shall outlive me.
Movement so smooth you are almost feline.
Beauty so great you're a joy to behold.
You can never leave me, for you are mine.
Inside you're so hot, yet outside so cold.
Sometimes I see you and wonder why me?
Was I blessed by God when I got this ring?
True, the ring of our wedlock is a key,
Yet still I adore you, but for one thing:
So smooth and so fresh and so young you are,
Would that you were a woman, not a car!

Darius Bazergan

i) Look through the poem to find 'typical' vocabulary used for love poetry.
ii) Rewrite the last line of the poem.
iii) Choose *one* of the following:
- rewrite the poem as a letter to an agony column;
- write your own poem which tricks the reader's expectations in a similar way to 'Italian Beauty'.

The following poems play on our knowledge of advertising to make a point about the lifestyles of women and men, and the way in which they are influenced by advertising. Read through the poems and answer the questions which follow.

Advertisement

The lady takes *The Times* and *Vogue*,
Wears Dior dresses, Gucci shoes,
Puts fresh-cut flowers round her room
And lots of carrots in her stews.

A moss-green Volvo, morning walks,
And holidays in Guadeloupe;
Long winter evenings by the fire
With Proust and cream of carrot soup.

Raw carrots on a summer lawn,
Champagne, a Gioconda smile;
Glazed carrots in a silver dish
For Sunday lunch. They call it style.

Wendy Cope

Tonight We Will Fake Love

Tonight, we will
fake love together.
You my love, possess
all the essential qualities
as listed by *Playboy*.
You will last me for
as long as two weeks
or until such a time
as your face & figure
go out of fashion.
I will hold you close
to my Hollywood-standard body,
the smell of which
has been approved
by my ten best friends
and a representative
of Lifebuoy.
I will prop my paperback
Kama Sutra
on the dressing table
& like programmed souls
we will perform
& like human beings
we will grow tired
of our artificially sweetened
diluted & ready to drink
love affairs.

Steve Turner

think What do the advertisements and poems say about the characteristics of the 'perfect' woman? Make a list of them. What might be seen as the characteristics of the perfect man?

choose

a Some advertisements make their customers feel inadequate. Look at the 'Dumpy to Dazzling' advertisement and rewrite it to sell the product without making the customer feel inadequate.

p169 ▷ **b** Carry out a survey in your class to find out which advertisement in the press or on the television/cinema screen is currently the most popular, and why. Then prepare a talk for the group explaining why you feel these particular adverts appeal to your group.

p152 ▷ **c** Select four adverts from the media in which men are used to advertise a product, or, in which the products are intended to be bought by men. In what ways are men and boys over-simplified, glamourized, degraded or persuaded by these advertisements? Do you think women and men are equally exploited by advertising? Write your ideas down in essay form.

extra Ownership and bias

Newspapers are sponsored by individuals or groups who normally have some political allegiance. This may mean that articles are written with a certain bias or favouritism.

The following articles are taken from the front page of *The Independent* the *Daily Telegraph* and *The Guardian* on Monday 23rd February. Read them through carefully, and try to decide which political party the papers may favour.

The Independent

French seize four left-wing extremists

Jean-Marc Rouillan.

From Patrick Marnham in Paris

FRENCH police have arrested four of the leading members of the Marxist terrorist organisation *Action Directe.*

The arrests were carried out after an attack on a farm in the smallvillage of le Gué-Girault, 13 miles outside Orleans.

Members of RAID (the French police special intervention group) blew down the front door of the farm at 9.50 on Saturday night. When two men attempted to jump from a window they were stopped with machine gun fire. All four of the people inside then surrendered.

They proved to be Jean-Marc Rouillan, Nathalie Menigon, Joelle Aubron and Bernard Cipriani. Nathalie Menigon and

Joelle Aúberon are the two women wanted for the murder of Georges Besse, then head of Renault, outside his Paris home last November. Mr Rouillan is the head of the organisation. Mr Cipriani was his bodyguard.

Inside the farm, police found an arsenal of weapons and explosives and a large sum in French francs and foreign currency.

Among the evidence found linking the occupants to the murder of Georges Besse was his briefcase. This had been cut into strips and Ms Menigon was using it to feed her numerous collection of pet hamsters.

One of the rooms in the farm is reported to have been fitted out as a court room for "a people's tribunal", in which the terrorists had intended to try a hostage who would be taken in exchange for Regis Schleicher, one of their members who is soon to be tried for the murder of two policemen.

A list of possible hostages was also found at the farm. Among the names of many prominent people was that of the press proprietor Robert Hersant who owns *Le Figaro* and many other newspapers.

The police also say that they have found extensive documen-

tary evidence linking *Action Directe* to the Red Brigades in Italy, the West German Red Army Faction and the Belgian *Cellules Communistes Combattantes.*

The arrests followed a tip-off received by the police four days ago and two informers are now entitled to share the one milion franc rewarded offered. in exchange for information by the Minister for Security, Robert Pandraud.

Following the arrests, President Mitterrand sent a message of congratulation to Jacques Chirac and Mr Chirac sent a similar message to Charles Pasqua and Mr Pandraud, the responsible ministers.

Nathalie Menigon.

Daily Telegraph

4 held in French terror coup

By John Izbicki in Paris

FRENCH police have arrested four suspected leading members of Action Directe, the outlawed anarchist group that has brought terror to the streets of France for seven years.

All four have been on the police wanted list concerning murder and bombings and have been on the run since 1982.

Nearly 70lb of high explosives and 80 detonators were taken away by police after the two men and two women were found in a secluded farmhouse near Orleans late on Saturday.

A cache of arms, including pistols and sub-machine guns was also discovered, along with large sums of money in French and other currencies, and a list of eminent persons in politics and business believed candidates for assassination or kidnapping.

This major police coup has given the Paris authorities some much-needed relief, for it has come on the eve of the trial opening in the capital's Assizes today of Georges Ibrahim Abdallah, believed to be the European leader of FARL – the Lebanese Armed Revolutionary Faction.

Security has been tightened, and the 3,500 special riot police patrolling Paris streets are on a "red alert" for trouble.

The arrests, in a village 84 miles south of Paris, have been considered so great a coup that President Mitterrand and M Chirac, Prime Minister, sent personal greetings telegrams yesterday to Chief Inspector Ange Mancini, the man chiefly responsible for the arrests.

His "raid" force (the special "search, assist, intervene and dissuade" police section, often used in tricky operations and

Continued on Back Page, Col. 4

The Guardian

Leaders of Action Directe terrorist group seized

Jean-Marc Rouillan —
farmhouse arrest

From Campbell Page in Paris

Police struck a decisive blow against the French terrorist group Action Directe when they arrested the two founders and two senior members of the extreme leftwing organisation in a remote farmhouse 20 miles from Orleans at the weekend.

Police found the terrorists had prepared "a people's prison" in the building for a hostage whom they intended to seize and use to secure the release of one of their associates, Regis Schleicher, who is in custody charged with the killing of two policemen in 1983.

Police also found in their Saturday night swoop the briefcase carried by the head of the Renault car company, Mr Georges Besse, when he was shot dead in a Paris street in November. There were also photocopies of documents from the briefcase, and stocks of arms and explosives.

The four terrorists, Jean-Marc Rouillan, aged 34, his companion, Nathalie Menigon, aged 29, Georges Cipriani, aged 35, and Joelle Aubron, aged 27, who is Schleicher's wife, were members of the international wing of Action Directe.

This section forged links with Italian and Belgian terrorist groups and with the West German Red Army Faction and plunged into terrorism and political assassinations across Europe. When a senior French Defence Ministry official, Rene Audran, was killed in January, 1985, Action Directe and the Red Army Faction claimed joint responsibility.

Action Directe claimed sole responsibility for the Besse shooting, but the operation fitted into a pattern of attacks against symbolic European industrial figures.

Posters carrying photographs of Menigon and Aubron were distributed throughout France after the Besse killing, which was believed to be the work of two women. The French authorities, which broke fresh ground by offering rewards for useful information about Middle East terrorism in France last year, made a similar offer after his killing. It apparently produced results.

After 36 hours' surveillance in the snow-covered countryside police were ordered into action on Saturday night. The four were sitting down to dinner when the police let off an explosive charge at the door and rushed in before they could reach for their weapons.

Villagers were astonished to discover that the four were terrorist. A woman who sold milk, eggs and chickens to Menigon described her as charming, and a man even asked them to keep an eye on his house while he was away.

The four were being questioned in Versailles yesterday about the murder of Audran and the attempted killing of a senior official in the National Employers' Organisation.

think

1 Pick out any factual differences between the articles.
2 Are there any differences in tone put across in the pictures and their titles, and in the headlines?
3 Examining the articles carefully, try to decide if there is any evidence of bias.
4 Which article do you prefer and why?

choose

p152

a Write an essay comparing the articles and focusing on the differences between them. Try to explain why the differences may appear, and take into consideration the journalist's intention and the expected readership.

b *The Independent* was launched in 1986 on a wave of publicity stressing its independence from political or ownership bias. Look again at the article from *The Independent* and compare it with the articles from *The Guardian* and *The Daily Telegraph*. In what ways (if any) is *The Independent* different in its approach from the other two papers?

p175

c Carry out some research to find out who owns each of the major papers on the market now. Devise a questionnaire for the class to complete, to see how many of them know where each paper's political allegiance lies. Then prepare a talk discussing your results.

Changing Society

starter School

Has education changed society or does society change education? Whichever way round it is, teaching styles are very different now from 100 years ago, and the demands on teachers are also very different. Below is an article written by a teacher, describing the job as she sees it. Read it through carefully and then answer the questions which follow.

Could You pass the Teacher Test?

'People who can, do. People who can't, teach.' That was what I was told in the early Seventies when I was considering my job options. Then, as now, teaching had little status as a profession. You went into it if you didn't think you were bright enough for University. If you went to University and *still* didn't know what to do when you graduated you could always become a teacher. After all, anybody could teach, couldn't they? There was nothing to it. If you had half an ounce of personality, a head full of facts and enough idealism to see you through when the going got rough you might even succeed in being remembered by a handful of ex-dunderheads as someone who changed their lives for the better. At least it was 'something to fall back on' regular salary, nice long holidays, hours that would fit well later on with family life. Like marrying the boy-next-door, teaching was guaranteed to please your mum and dad. And it was worthwhile.

However, it's not advisable just to drift into teaching because you can't think of anything else to do. It takes guts and commitment to be a teacher. It certainly isn't easy work. And the first thing you need is a very positive idea of what you, as an individual, have to offer the profession.

Like so many others, I was drawn to teaching partly because I thought I could do better than most of the teachers who bored me to death during my own education, and partly because of the inspiration of one excellent history teacher who was so in love with Elizabeth I, as a woman, that we adolescent girls were mesmerised.

However, affection for your subject, even the ability to communicate your knowledge, is not enough to be a good teacher, and this is one of the first things you learn during your training.

Throughout your probationary year in your first job you are rigorously assessed

and this can be very tough. If you're used to being examined on your knowledge of your own subject alone it can come as a shock to be examined on your *human* skills as well; your 'relationship with other staff and pupils', for example, or your 'attitude to criticism and advice'.

A secondary school teacher takes around 25 classes a week and, before these lessons can begin, she's likely to have to quell exuberant chatter about Dirty Den and Angie or the latest line in Nikes. If she succeeds in getting the class to settle down, there are always interruptions to deal with – rubbers flicked, pencils lost, kids who turn their Bunsen burners into Rambo flame throwers, and the ones who subtly insnare you in irrelevant debates.

At its worst a teacher also has to deal with apathy, defiance, and even outright abuse . . . with time, experience and ingenuity she's developed numerous flexible strategies to cope. She's learnt, for example, how to beguile the disaffected with accusations that they're spoiling their own friends' enjoyment of the lesson. She's also learned how best to use humour, when it's appropriate to ignore what's going on, when and *how* to exert authority in a way that's not counter productive to the actual learning taking place. And much, much more.

Alone in front of a class a teacher hopes to be creative and inspired. Like a performer, she has to be charismatic, even at nine in the morning, magically turning dry text *and* her improvisations into something that can grip an audience. But *unlike* an actress, she also has to be her own administrator, and being brilliant in the classroom counts for little if she's inefficient in the more mundane aspects of the job.

She also has to be a social worker. Often seen as society's scapegoat for everything from drugs to unemployment, she is, of course, no more to blame for all this than an orchestral conductor is to blame for the dissonance of modern music. But she still has to *deal* with all the personal problems of her pupils – and it's not only in Primary schools that a teacher has to stand in for mother and mop up tears.

Even at its best, actual teaching accounts for a relatively small part of the job. Down at the chalk face, as one teacher says, 'You're often little more than a policewoman trying to keep the kids off the streets.'

Gillian Capper

think

1 Why, according to the article, do most teachers join the profession?
2 In what ways does the job appear to be similar to that of a policewoman or an actress?

choose

a Using the information given in the article above, write Gillian Capper's diary for an average day at school.
b Compare the situation in the school described in the article to the situation in your school. Is this an accurate description of schools? Write your own report, stating your views on the skills needed by, *either* teachers *or* pupils in the modern education system.

p175 c Find out about the job of the teacher at the turn of the century. To what extent is the job different today? Present your findings in a factual oral or written report.

p161

1 Changing roles

The following extract is taken from Mary Stott's autobiography, *Forgetting's No Excuse*. Read it through carefully and then answer the questions below.

'The strands of my life cannot be separated out: it is their interlocking, heredity and environment, work and home, that makes the pattern. Being a journalist's child made me a journalist; having a working mother made me expect to go on working myself; being born female hindered me from becoming the sort of newspaper journalist I would have liked to be; being a wife and mother probably made me a more effective woman's page editor.'

think

1 Mary Stott describes her feelings about herself in terms of upbringing and gender. How does she believe her gender has helped and hindered her?
2 Put into your own words the meaning of 'heredity and environment, work and home' in the context of the passage.
3 Make a list of:
- things,
- people,
- events,

which have influenced you. Think about other families – do they seem to have followed their parents in terms of their interests and skills? Think about your own brothers and sisters – are they treated differently because of their gender? Write your own short description of the influences on your life (under 100 words). This can be used as the basis of an oral presentation or discussion.

p175 ⟹

Changing roles for women is a common theme in society today, but it is not just the position of women that has changed. As many women take on traditionally male roles, many men take on those roles which are traditionally female. Yet in many cases men and women who begin to break the role are labelled as incapable of performing the new task.

Below is a list of rather stereotyped attitudes about gender. Use them to decide what your own views are. Some suggest that men and women are different and should be treated differently, and others suggest that equality means uniform similarity. What do you think?

If women aren't permitted to go out to work they are stifled and unfulfilled.

Women are efficient organizers.

A woman's place is in the home.

Men don't make good 'housewives'.

Men are in control of the office.

If men and women are to be equal they must be allowed an equal stab at employment and house management.

Men have the right to raise their children.

Men are men and women are women, they should stick to what they're good at.

Men at work loose contact with the home.

Men are just as sensitive as women.

Women at work are bossy.

Sexual equality means the freedom to choose how you live your life.

Now write a 200 word account of your views on male and female roles.

Below are three poems about the position of women. Read them through and then answer the questions which follow.

from: **Maintenance Engineer**

One Friday night it happened, soon after we were wed,
My old man came in from work as usual I said:
'Your tea is on the table, clean clothes are on the rack.
Your bath will soon be ready, I'll come up and scrub your back.'
He kissed me very tenderly and said, 'I'll tell you flat
The service I give my machine ain't half as good as that.'
I said . . .

Chorus
I'm not your little woman, your sweetheart or your dear
I'm a wage slave without wages, I'm a maintenance engineer.

Well then we got to talking. I told him how I felt,
How I keep him running just as smooth as some conveyor belt!
Well after all, it's I'm the one provides the power supply
He goes just like the clappers on me steak and kidney pie.
His fittings are all shining 'cos I keep 'em nice and clean
And he tells me his machine tool is the best I've ever seen.
But . . .

Chorus
I'm not your little woman, your sweetheart or your dear
I'm a wage slave without wages, I'm a maintenance engineer.

Sandra Kay

I Had Rather Be A Woman

I had rather be a woman
Than an earwig
But there's not much in it sometimes.
We both crawl out of bed
But there the likeness ends.
Earwigs don't have to
Feed the children,
Feed the cat,
Feed the rabbits,
Feed the dishwasher.
They don't need
Clean sheets,
Clean clothes,
Clean carpets,
A clean bill of health.
They just rummage about
In chrysanthemums.
No-one expects them
To have their
Teetotal, vegetarian
Mothers-in-law
To stay for Christmas,
Or to feel a secret thrill
At the thought of extending the kitchen.
Earwigs can snap their pincers at life
And scurry about being quite irresponsible.
They enjoy an undeserved reputation
Which frightens the boldest child.
Next time I feel hysterical
I'll bite a hole in a dahlia.

Daphne Schiller

The Washerwoman

She washes her old man's dirty clothes,
her son's dirty clothes,
her daughter's dirty clothes.

Inhumanly clean
like her murdered life
she wipes away at times the sinful tear of a dream
with her clean
washerwoman's hands.

Anna Swir

1 Discuss with a partner the possible meanings of the following words and phrases:
- 'I'm a wage slave without wages, I'm a maintenance engineer.' *(Maintenance Engineer)*
- 'A clean bill of health.' 'an undeserved reputation' 'Hysterical' *(I Had Rather Be A Woman)*
- 'Inhumanly clean.' 'she wipes away at times the sinful tear of a dream' *(The Washerwoman)*

2 Write a list of the emotions which the writers might have been experiencing as they wrote the poems, e.g. anger, sadness, determination.

3 Have you ever experienced gender prejudice? Discuss the experience with a partner.

a Write a poem about the position of men or women in past, present or future society.

b Write a short story involving gender prejudice.

c Design a series of advertisements encouraging women into business management, or men into a child-minding scheme.

d Use the following statements as the basis for oral discussion:
- 'Men make better parents.'
- 'In order that society remains stable, women should remain in the home.'
- 'There should be a Minister for Women.'

p169 ⇨

2

Living through changes

As a society changes people are forced to adapt and develop, but how far can humans adapt? In *Brother in the Land* Robert Swindells describes the way in which one family lives through the changes brought about by a nuclear conflict. Read through this extract taken from the beginning of the book and then answer the questions.

East is East and West is West, and maybe it was a difference of opinion or just a computer malfunction. Either way, it set off a chain of events that nobody but a madman could have wanted and which nobody, not even the madmen could stop.

There were missiles.
Under the earth.
In the sky.
Beneath the waves.
Missiles with thermo-nuclear warheads, enough to kill everybody on earth.
Three times over.

And something set them off: sent them flying. West to East and East to West, crossing in the middle like cars on a cable railway.

East and West, the sirens wailed. Emergency procedures began, hampered here and there by understandable panic. Helpful leaflets were distributed and sealed off. V.I.P.'s went to their bunkers and volunteers stood at their posts. Suddenly nobody wanted to be an engine-driver anymore, or a model or a rock star. Everybody wanted to be one thing: a survivor. But it was an overcrowded profession.

The missiles climbed their trajectory arcs, rolled over the top and came down, accelerating. Below everyone was ready. The Frimleys had their shelter in the lounge. The Bukovskys favoured the cellar. A quick survey would have revealed no over whelming preference, worldwide, for one part of the house over the other.

Down came the missiles. Some had just one warhead, others had several, ranging from the compact, almost tactical warhead to the large, family size. Every town was to receive its own, individually-programmed warhead. Not one had been left out.

They struck, screaming in with pinpoint accuracy, bursting with blinding flashes, brighter than a thousand suns. Whole towns and city-centres vapourised instantly; while tarmac, trees and houses thirty miles from the explosions burst into flames. Fireballs, expanding in a second to several miles across, melted and devoured all matter that fell within their diameters. Blast-waves, travelling faster than sound, ripped through the suburbs. Houses disintegrated and vanished. So fierce were the flames that they devoured all the oxygen around them, suffocating those people who took refuge in deep shelters. Winds of a hundred-and-fifty miles an hour, rushing in to fill the vacuum, created fire-storms and howled through the streets, where temperatures in their thousands cooked the subterranean dead. The very earth heaved and shook as the warheads rained down, burst upon burst upon burst, and a terrible thunder rent the skies.

For an hour the warheads fell, then ceased. A great silence descended over the land. The Bukovskys had gone, and the Frimleys were no more. Through the silence, through the pall of smoke and dust that blackened the sky, trillions of deadly radioactive particles began to fall. They fell soundlessly, settling like invisible snow on the devastated earth.

Incredibly, here and there, people had survived the bombardment. They lay stunned in their ruins, incapable of thought. Drifting on the wind, the particles sifted in upon them, landing unseen on clothing, skin and hair, so that most of these too would die, but slowly.

Most, but not all. There were those whose fate it was to wander this landscape of poisonous desolation. One of them was me.

Robert Swindells

think

1 Select three phrases or images from the passage which you find particularly striking, and explain why they stand out and are important for you.
2 Why do you think the writer uses the words 'East' and 'West' so frequently?
3 Why are the names of the two families ('Bukovsky' and 'Frimley') important?
4 Look at the style of writing. Why do you think the author chooses:
   ● short paragraphs;
   ● short sentences;
   ● technical vocabulary?

choose

a Carry out a role play of the story teller's meeting with another survivor.
b Imagine you are the person speaking in the extract. Carry on your story.
c Find out from your local Town Hall what provisions there are for aid or survival in the event of a local or national disaster, (flooding, an industrial accident on a large scale,

p168 ▷ a nuclear attack). Write a report of your findings and give an oral presentation to the class.

d   Imagine you are having to survive in very difficult circumstances, and that you have only the company of your best friend. Write up an account of your survival paying close attention to the effect of the disaster on your friendship. Think hard about your own personality and that of your friend. What would you value in their character? What might annoy you and place further stress on the situation? It's best to choose a real person as your friend in the story (though you can give them a made up name). Be as honest as you can about your friend and yourself!

One of the most common subjects which arises, when the changing society becomes a topic of conversation, is inflation. Older people may make comments such as: 'Things cost more than they used to', 'in my day you could buy a pound of sugar for . . .' The pictures which follow show how prices have changed this century. Take a look at them carefully.

N.B.: 1p = 2.4 d.   28g = 1 oz   0.6 litre = 1 pint

What £1 bought in 1914
4 pints Whitbread's beer 10d.
1 lb 2oz Brooke Bond tea 1/8¼d.
3¾ pints milk 3¾d.
1½ lb shin of beef 1/3d.
2 lb sugar 4d.
1½ oz wool 9d.
40 Woodbines 8d.
5 oz Nosegay tobacco 1/10½d.
½ lb cheddar cheese 5½d.
2¾ cwt coal 3/6d.
¼ bt Johnny Walker whisky 1/1d.
2½ loaves bread 7½d.
6 pr cotton socks 3/–d.
3 lb rice 7½d.
3 lb potatoes 2¼d.
9 oz chocolate 1/1½d.
¾ lb butter 10½d.
4 eggs 5d.
1¾ bars soap 5½d.
Total £1.0.0¾d.

What £1 bought in 1934
1½ pints beer 10½d.
¾ lb Brooke Bond tea 1/9.
1 pt milk 3½d.
1½ lb rice 3¾d.
1½ lb sugar 3¾d.
1 oz wool 10d.
20 Woodbines 8d.
2¼ oz Nosegay tobacco 1/10½d.
½ lb cheese 5½d.
1½ cwt coal 3/4½d.
3 nips Johnny Walker whisky 3/2d.
2 loaves bread 7½d.
3 pr cotton socks 3/–
1 lb shin of beef 1/3d.
3 lb potatoes 2¼d.
12 oz chocolate 1/–d.
¾ lb butter 10½d.
2½ eggs 5d.
1 bar soap 5d.
Total £1.0.0¼d.

What £1 bought in 1954

½ pint beer 10½d.
¼ lb Brooke Bond tea 1/8d.
½ pt milk 3¾d.
½ lb rice 7½d.
½ lb sugar 3¾d.
½ oz wool 8½d.
5 Woodbines cigarettes 8d.
½ oz tobacco 1/10½d.
¼ lb cheese 5½d.
½ cwt coal 3/6
1 nip Johnny Walker whisky 1/1d.
1 loaf bread 7½d.
1 pr socks 2/4d.
1 lb shin of beef 1/4d.
1 lb potatoes 2d.
¼ lb chocolate 1/–d.
¼ lb butter 11d.
1 egg 5d.
½ bar soap 5½d.
Total £1.0.0.

think

1 Make your own list of what items you could buy for a pound today.
2 Which items have increased the most in price?
3 Note down some items which have increased in price a great deal in your life time.

choose

a Using the lists above, write a factual account of how prices went up between 1914 and 1954. Use historical sources to try to suggest why the prices altered as they did.
b Find out how much each of the items listed in 1914, would cost today. Record your information in the same layout as you see above, and state what the total bill would be.
c Imagine you are the person doing the household shopping in one of the pictures above. Work with a partner to produce a role play of a shopping trip. Then imagine that those characters have been transported into a modern supermarket, and carry on the role play.

p174 ▷

3

Losses and gains

A changing society moves from the old and develops the new, and as it does so there are always losses and gains. One of the most obvious changes is the further development of science: cures for diseases that previously killed, the use of drugs to moderate the effect of illnesses and to relieve pain. But as medicines are used in hospitals so they are misused in wider society.

The extract below is taken from a newspaper report on drug abuse and the picture from a series of health education advertisements. Both deal with heroin addiction. Read them through carefully and then answer the questions which follow.

Chasing the Dragon

Gary began using heroin shortly before his 16th birthday, when he was still at school. Nobody realised because the only overt clues were slender strips of scorched aluminium foil which his mother found hidden under his bed. 'Who could know what it was for,' she says.

She knows now. Gary lays a trail of the purest heroin he can buy on to the foil and heats it from underneath with a lighted match. The powder turns into a bead of black liquid which runs down the foil. Gary pursues it with a tube through which he inhales the pungent fumes – 'chasing the dragon'.

By the time his mother realised the truth it was too late. 'Chasing' heroin may be marginally safer than injecting, but the end result is the same. Now 18, Gary is addicted. He needs five or six packets – 'ching bags' in the jargon – a day just to keep the withdrawal symptoms at bay, otherwise 'the pains come back and my eyes start dribbling and I feel sick all the time,' he says.

Feeding that addiction costs at least £200 a week, which Gary gets by stealing and petty fraud. 'He's become a liar and would do anything for money,' says his mother. Unable to cope, she has moved out of their council flat in south-east London just to get away from him: 'I don't want to see him any more.'

Gary's weight is now down to just over six stone, his face is covered from his constant scratching – and he is in constant trouble with the police. He has no prospects whatsoever. The heroin used to provide a panacea, but 'I don't get a buzz any more,' he says, and the likelihood is that he will soon begin injecting the drug into his veins, for more immediate effect. He knows how easy it would be: 'There's a bloke round the corner who'll stick the needle in for you if you're scared – for a consideration, of course.'

There are thousands of boys – and girls – like Gary in south-east London. . . On the estates in north Southwark alone, on either side of the Old Kent Road, there are reckoned to be 1,000 regular young users of heroin. According to Ronno Griffiths, co-ordinator of the borough's drug project: 'We're not talking about a group of deviant characters who you'd expect to get involved in this sort of thing, but very ordinary kids who are incorporating heroin into their lives and subculture.'

Tony Moss (The Observer)

think

1 What are the main differences between 'chasing the dragon' and injecting heroin?
2 Highlight the 10 most significant things about Gary's addiction.

3 Why do you think people take heroin?

4 Do you think the advertisement pictured here would put young people off taking heroin? Discuss your opinions with a partner.

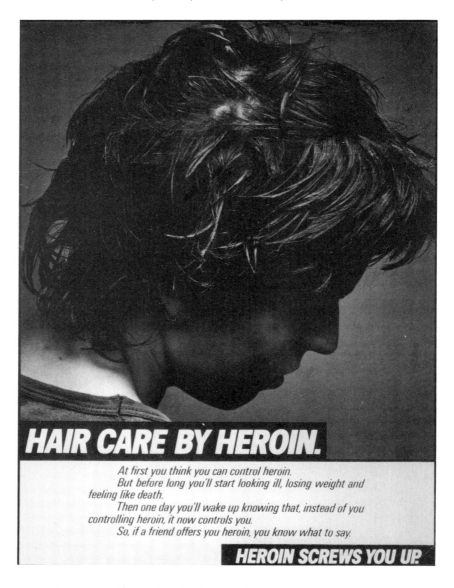

HAIR CARE BY HEROIN.

At first you think you can control heroin.
But before long you'll start looking ill, losing weight and feeling like death.
Then one day you'll wake up knowing that, instead of you controlling heroin, it now controls you.
So, if a friend offers you heroin, you know what to say.

HEROIN SCREWS YOU UP.

choose

a Using the information in the article and advertisement, write a concise and factual account of the likely effects of taking heroin.

b Write the story of how another individual gets involved in taking drugs. This could be based on a real or imagined situation.

c Work with a partner to develop a role play involving the characters in the story. Act out three significant points in their lives. You might choose:

- the first time Gary is offered heroin;
- the time when Gary's mother first discovers he takes heroin;
- Gary and his mother going to a specialist for help.

d Design a series of advertisements, or write a script for a TV advertisement, to persuade young people against taking heroin. You will need to provide notes to go with the advertisements in order to explain them fully.

p174 ⟶

Sometimes societies change when one civilization defeats another in battle, but even then the conquerors may not be entirely happy with the changes. The following poem tells of the victors of such a battle, looking at the battlefield. They know they are successful and yet they feel rather differently.

Conquerors

By sundown we came to a hidden village
Where all the air was still
And no sound met our tired ears, save
For the sorry drip of rain from blackened trees
And the melancholy song of swinging gates.
Then through a broken pane some of us saw
A dead bird in a rustling cage, still
Pressing his tattered breast against the bars,
His beak wide open. And
As we hurried through the weed-grown street,
A gaunt dog started up from some dark place
And shambled off on legs as thin as sticks
Into the wood to die at least in peace.
No one had told us that victory was like this;
Not one amongst us would have eaten bread
Before he'd filled the mouth of every grey child
That sprawled, stiff as stone, before the shattered door.
There was not one who did not think of home.

Henry Treece

 think

1 Decide on one phrase which you think is the most important to the poem, and give reasons for your choice.
2 Why do you think the poet chooses to describe a bird, a dog and a child in detail?
3 What do you think has happened to cause this scene?

 **choose**

p174

a Carry out some role play of a conversation two of the victors might have had:
  ● before the battle;
  ● after the battle.
b The poem describes the losses and gains of victory in battle. Describe another situation where you, or a character of your invention, have won something but have mixed feelings about it.

p154

c The poet is shocked by what he sees and, in turn, shocks the reader. Write your own description of a scene which would shock you, trying at the same time to pass on your feeling of shock to the reader.
d Drawing on the whole of this section, write your own story entitled 'Losses and Gains'.

extra **Living on**

The two poems which follow reveal how parents can hold wishes for their children's future, which enable them to come to terms with their own old age and to cope with the changing society in which they live. Read them through and then answer the questions.

Sonnet 2
When forty winters shall beseige thy brow,
And dig deep trenches in thy beauty's field,
Thy youth's proud livery, so gazed on now,
Will be a totter'd weed, of small worth held:
Then being ask'd where all thy beauty lies,
Where all the treasures of thy lusty days;
To say, within thy own deep sunken eyes,
Were an all-eating shame and thriftless praise.
How much more praise deserved thy beauty's use.
If thou couldst answer, 'This fair child of mine
Shall sum my count, and make my old excuse,'
Proving his beauty by succession thine!
This is to be new made when thou art old,
And see thy blood warm when thou feel'st it cold.

William Shakespeare

The Child at the Window

Remember this when childhood's far away;
The sunlight of a showery first spring day;
You from your house-top window laughing down;
And I, returned with whip-cracks from a ride,
On the great lawn below you, playing the clown.
Time blots our gladness out. Let this with love abide. . .

The brave March day; and you, not four years old,
Up in your nursery world – all heaven for me.
Remember this – the happiness I hold –
In far off springs I shall not live to see;
The world one map of wastening war unrolled,
And you, unconscious of it, setting my spirit free.

For you must learn, beyond bewildering years,
How little things beloved and held are best.
The windows of the world are blurred with tears,
And troubles come like cloud-banks from the west.
Remember this, some afternoon in spring,
When your own child looks down and makes your sad heart sing.

Siegfried Sassoon

think

1 In what ways are youth and age contrasted in the poems?
2 In 'Sonnet 2' Shakespeare uses various images to show how people age. Pick out those words and phrases which compare the changes in the body to changes in the landscape.
3 Growing older is a change which everyone will experience. Even if the society we live in changes little, we still have to adapt. Discuss with a partner some of the changes of life style people have to make as they grow old.
4 Which poem do you prefer and why?

choose

a Both of the poems are addressed to a particular person. Work out who that person is and then write the reply which they might write to the poem. Your reply can be in the form of a letter or poem.
b The first poem is a sonnet; a fourteen line poem, with a regular rhyming scheme and ten beats to the line. Write your own sonnet on the topic of changing society.
c Both poems create much of their effect by controlling the sounds in the poem. Both Shakespeare and Sassoon use alliteration;
  ● 'This fair child of **m**ine shall sum **m**y count, and **m**ake **m**y old excuse,'
  ● 'The **w**indows of the **w**orld'
  and repetition:
  ● 'deep',
  ● 'beauty'
  ● 'Remember this'
  to create the feeling of an echo. Write your own piece of prose or poetry in which you use alliteration and repetition to create a particular overall effect.

p156 **d** What wishes would you have for your child, if you had one, in our present society? Write a letter or a poem to your imagined child to pass on your feelings.

starter   **Imagination**

Read through the following poem, look at the picture, and then answer the questions which follow.

The key of the kingdom
When we were children,
We possessed the key to a kingdom
Such as this world has yet to see.
Wherever we went;
By lakes,
Pools
And Streams,
In woods,
Meadows
And fields,
There was a world beyond belief
In which anything could be something else.
A world
Whose every corner
Would yield some new adventure or surprise.
A world
In which we ruled
And was ours alone.

Only we children had the key,
The key of the kingdom.

A world inhabited by goblins, ghosts and ghouls,
Dragons, trolls, witches, sorcerers,
Knights, fair damsels, wicked kings,
And green-skinned, three-eyed floops.
A world of enchanted geography
Magic Forests,
Glass mountains
And fountains of youth.

In this world
We held our castles
Made of TV boxes,
Against marauding bands of Vikings
Armed with swords made of lattice
And shields taken from the tops of garbage cans.
We sailed with Columbus
Across the unchartered waters of a lily-pond,
We decended.
With Captain Nemo
To 20,000 leagues beneath the bathwater.
We went west with the pioneers

By coaster wagon,
And to the East with Marco Polo
By tricycle.
We defied savage Indians
From the next block
And returned alive
In time for an afternoon nap.

We hunted fierce man-eating squirrels,
We dared damnation
By taking the trainer wheels
Off our first bicycle.
We did a zillion billion other brave
Courageous
Bold
Fun things.

Now that we are older,
Wiser
And more mature
This kingdom no longer has our allegiance.
We have lost the key,
And it has perished with the rust of misuse
And neglect.
Age is the grave yard
Of all our youthful hopes.
Dreams
and Experiences.

Edward Reed

1 What does Edward Reed see as the difference between childhood and adulthood?
2 Where do most of the images of childhood fantasy come from?
3 What is meant by 'the key to the kingdom'?
4 This poem is about:
  - remembering childhood;
  - lost innocence;
  - our lack of control over our imagination;
  - a child's view of life;
  - a child's imagination.

Discuss these statements with a partner and decide which you agree and disagree with.

choose

p152

a A child's imagination is seen as a precious gift in this poem, but do you think children have better imaginations than adults? Write an argumentative essay *either* for *or* against this view.
b This is a very idealistic view of childhood. Write your own poem which *either* shows a less positive view of childhood, *or* shows a positive view of adulthood.

1 Different types of fantasy

Fantasy fiction comes in many forms, from science fiction to comic strips. In the short story below certain words and phrases have been highlighted (in italics) as being typical of science fiction writing. Underneath the story is a list of categories which are often found in science fiction writing. Match the highlighted words to the appropriate categories and then answer the questions which follow.

The Pedestrian

To enter out into that silence that was the city at eight o'clock of a misty evening in November, to put your feet upon that buckling concrete walk, to step over grassy seams and make your way, hands in pockets, through the silences, that was what Mr Leonard Mead most dearly loved to do. He would stand upon the corner of an intersection and peer down long moonlit avenues of sidewalk in four directions, deciding which way to go, but it really made no difference; *he was alone in this world of 2053 A.D.*, or as good as alone, and with a final decision made, a path selected, he would stride off, sending patterns of frosty air before him like the smoke of a cigar.

Sometimes he would walk for hours and miles and return only at midnight to his house. And on his way he would see the cottages and homes with their dark windows, and it was not unequal to walking through a graveyard where only the faintest glimmers of firefly light appeared in flickers behind the windows. Sudden gray phantoms seemed to manifest upon inner room walls where a curtain was still undrawn against the night, or there were whisperings and murmurs where a window in a tomb-like building was still open.

Mr Leonard Mead would pause, cock his head, listen, look, and march on, his feet making no noise on the lumpy walk. For long ago he had wisely changed to sneakers when strolling at night, because the dogs in intermittent squads would parallel his journey with barkings if he wore hard heels, and lights might click on and faces appear and an entire street be startled by the passing of a lone figure, himself, in the early November evening.

On this particular evening he began his journey in a westerly direction, toward the hidden sea. There was a good crystal frost in the air; it cut the nose and made the lungs blaze like a Christmas tree inside; you could feel the cold light going on and off, all the branches filled with invisible snow. He listened to the faint push of his soft shoes through autumn leaves with satisfaction, and whistled a cold quiet whistle between his teeth, occasionally picking up a leaf as he passed, examining its skeletal pattern in the infrequent lamplights as he went on, smelling its rusty smell.

'Hello, in there,' he whispered to every house on every side as he moved. *'What up tonight on Channel 4, Channel 7, Channel 9?* Where are the cowboys rushing, and do I see the United States Cavalry over the next hill to the rescue?' The street was silent and long and empty, with only his shadow moving like the shadow of a hawk in mid-country. If he closed his eyes and stood very still, frozen, he could imagine himself upon the center of a plain, a wintry, windless Arizona desert with no house in a thousand miles, and only dry river beds, the street, for company.

'What is it now?' he asked the houses, noticing his wrist watch. 'Eight-thirty

P.M.? Time for a dozen assorted murders? A quiz? A revue? A comedian falling off the stage?'

Was that a murmur of laughter from within a moon-white house? He hesitated, but went on when nothing more happened. He stumbled over a particularly uneven section of sidewalk. The cement was vanishing under flowers and grass. In ten years of walking by night or day, for thousands of miles, he had never met another person walking, not one in all that time.

He came to a cloverleaf intersection which stood silent where two main highways crossed the town. During the day it was a thunderous surge of cars, the gas stations open, a great insect rustling and a ceaseless jockeying for position as the scarab-beetles, a faint incense puttering from their exhausts, skimmed homeward to the far directions. But now these highways, too, were like streams in a dry season, all stone and bed and moon radiance.

He turned back on a side street, circling around toward his home. He was within a block of his destination when the lone car turned a corner quite suddenly and *flashed a fierce white cone of light upon him.* He stood entranced, not unlike a night moth, stunned by the illumination, and then drawn toward it.

A *metallic voice* called to him:

'Stand still. Stay where you are! Don't move!'

He halted.

'Put up your hands!'

'But —' he said.

'Your hands up! Or we'll shoot!'

The police, of course, but what a rare, incredible thing; in a city of three million, there was only *one* police car left, wasn't that correct? Ever since a year ago, 2052, the election year, the force had been cut down from three cars to one. Crime was ebbing; there was no need now for the police, save for this one lone car wandering and wandering the empty streets.

'Your name?' said the police car in a metallic whisper. He couldn't see the men in it for the bright light in his eyes.

'Leonard Mead,' he said.

'Speak up!'

'Leonard Mead!'

'Business or profession?'

'I guess you'd call me a writer.'

'No profession,' said the police car, as if talking to itself. The light held him fixed, like a museum specimen, needle thrust through chest.

'You might say that,' said Mr Mead. He hadn't written in years. Magazines and books didn't sell any more. Everything went on in the tomb-like houses at night now, he thought, continuing his fancy. The tombs, ill-lit by television light, where the people sat like the dead, the gray or multi-coloured lights touching their faces, but never really touching them.

'No profession,' said the phonograph voice, hissing. 'What are you doing out?'

'Walking,' said Leonard Mead.

'Walking!'

'Just walking,' he said simply, but his face felt cold.

'Walking, just walking, walking?'

Yes, sir.'

'Walking where? For what?'

'Walking for air. Walking to *see.*'

'Your address!'

'Eleven South Saint James Street.'

'And there is air in your house, you have an air conditioner, Mr Mead?'

'Yes.'

'And you have a viewing screen in your house to see with?'

'No.'

'No?' There was a crackling quiet that in itself was an accusation.

'Are you married, Mr Mead?'

'No.'

'Not married,' said the police voice behind the fiery beam. The moon was high and clear among the stars and the houses were gray and silent.

'Nobody wanted me,' said Leonard Mead with a smile.

'Don't speak unless you're spoken to!'

Leonard Mead waited in the cold night.

'Just *walking*, Mr Mead?'

'Yes.'

'But you haven't explained for what purpose.'

'I explained; for air, and to see, and just to walk.'

'Have you done this often?'

'Every night for years.'

The police car sat in the center of the street with its *radio throat faintly humming.*

'Well, Mr Mead,' it said.

'Is that all?' he asked politely.

'Yes,' said the voice. 'Here.' *There was a sigh, a pop. The back door of the police car sprang wide.* 'Get in.'

'Wait a minute, I haven't done anything!'

'Get in.'

'I protest!'

'Mr Mead.'

He walked like a man suddenly drunk. As he passed the front window of the car he looked in. *As he had expected, there was no one in the front seat, no one in the car at all.*

'Get in.'

He put his hand to the door and peered into the back seat, which was a little cell, a little black jail with bars. It smelled of riveted steel. It smelled of harsh antiseptic; it smelled too clean and hard and metallic. There was nothing soft there.

'Now if you had a wife to give you an alibi,' said the iron voice. 'But —'

'Where are you taking me?'

The car hesitated, or rather gave a faint whirring click, as if information, somewhere, was dropping card by punch-slotted card under electric eyes. *'To the Psychiatric Center for Research on Regressive Tendencies.'*

He got in. The door shut with a soft thud. The police car rolled through the night avenues, flashing its dim lights ahead.

They passed one house on one street a moment later, one house in an entire city of houses that were dark, but this one particular house had all of its electric lights brightly lit, every window a loud yellow illumination, square and warm in the cool darkness.

'That's *my* house,' said Leonard Mead.

No one answered him.

The car moved down the empty river-bed streets and off away, leaving the empty streets with the empty sidewalks, and no sound and no motion all the rest of the chill November night.

Ray Bradbury

Typical elements in science fiction
- Machines which are advanced sufficiently to talk, but which lack humanity.
- A setting in the future.
- Present technology with more functions.
- People who lack human characteristics.
- Strict regimes which take to an extreme current practices.
- A different attitude towards certain aspects of society (the Arts).
- Some complex and invented vocabulary.

think

1 Pick out the words and phrases which describe the voice coming from the car. What makes it so unpleasant?

2 Pick out those phrases which suggest that Mr Mead is different from the average person in 2053 AD.

3 Which aspects of the story do you find the most nightmarish?

4 In what ways is the world described similar to the one you live in?

choose

a This short story is written in a science fiction genre. Keeping the basic story the same, write it in another genre. Other genres you might choose are romance, a western, a realistic thriller, a comic farce.

b What makes a science fiction story? Write your own report on the elements which are necessary to writing a good science fiction story. Draw on the ideas stated above, and on any other science fiction stories you have read. You may wish to carry this out as an extended piece, reading other short stories, and taking notes on common elements.

p146 ▷

c Write your own science fiction story, using the elements which you have highlighted in the story above.

The following extract is taken from a fantasy thriller called *I am The Cheese* by Robert Cormier. The book is divided into two elements; a present tense narration of Adam's trip to see his father, and a series of taped interviews between Adam and a psychoanalyst. As the two elements run together, the exciting story of Adam's life is revealed. Read the extract through carefully and answer the questions which follow.

I am about to get on my bike and leave the town of Carver forever when I spot the telephone booth down the street. At last. I lash my father's package to the basket and push the bike towards the booth. An old lady looks at me as I go by and she smiles at the *took* on my head. She has a hat on her head, too. It looks like a red flowerpot. Complete with flowers. I smile at her. I am happy suddenly. I will survive Carver and next comes Fleming and then Hookset and Belton Falls. There are long distances between Fleming and Hookset and then between Hookset and Belton Falls but this does not discourage me. I feel strong and resolute. I defeated the troublemakers in the lunchroom and I will defeat anyone else. But most of all, I am about to talk to Amy, to hear her voice again.

I fumble for change and insert the coin and the male operator comes on the line. I give him the number and go through all the rest of the routine and then the line is ringing, ringing. Please be home, Amy, please be home.

'Hello, hello.'

The voice is harsh and impatient: Mr Hertz's headline voice.

'Hello, may I speak to Amy?'

'Who is this?'

'Adam. Adam Farmer. I'd like to speak to Amy, please.'

'Amy who? There's no Amy here.'

The voice is not the headline voice of Mr Hertz, after all. This is not her father.

I see the three fellows from the lunchroom on the street. They are drifting in my direction. Two of them are walking side by side, slowly and leisurely but something threatening in their pace. The other one, Whipper, walks alone, ahead of them. I feel trapped in the booth. The bike is vulnerable, untied and unbolted outside the booth. And I have a wrong number.

'Listen,' the man on the phone begins. 'I've got the bug and I been hacking away all day and I finally doze off and then the phone rings . . .'

'I'm sorry,' I say.

And I slam down the phone. I don't like to hang up on people but the troublemakers are drifting closer and I have to get out of there. I'm sorry, Amy. I can't even get a telephone number right. I don't deserve you.

The boys are coming closer, slowly but

surely and menacingly, and I swing open the door of the booth and grab the bike. I run along beside the bike and then leap upon it. My feet engage the pedals and I pump away. I shoot through a red light and a car blows its horn at me but I am away, leaving Carver behind, leaving the troublemakers behind, but I don't feel brave anymore and my cheeks are wet even though it isn't raining.

TAPE OZK008 0930 date deleted T–A

A: The grey man.

T: One moment please. Let me sit, first.

A: The grey man.

T: You look positively excited. I have never seen you in such a state. This is good.

A: The grey man.

T: And who is this grey man?

A: I'm not sure. But he's important. It happened last night after I returned to my room. They gave me a pill. And I lay there, letting myself drift. Thinking of all the blank spots that have been filled in – Amy – the clues – and suddenly I remembered him.

T: And you call this person the grey man?

A: Yes. But only in my mind. That's what I always called him. The grey man.

T: And why was that?

A: I don't know. I'm not sure. But I think it's important. He's important.

T: In what way?

A: I can't tell yet. I'm not certain. But I think of him, what he looked like, and I know he's important, a real clue. I can feel it in my bones.

T: Tell me more.
   (3-second interval.)

A: I wish I could. But I can't.

T: Can't or won't?

A: Can't, won't? Don't you think I want to remember, that I want to know? All I know right now is that there was a man in the past, someone I referred to as the grey man, and I have a feeling he was important. In all that blankness, he's the only clue I've got.

T: Then rest easy, relax, let it come. Perhaps a pill . . .

A: No, no pill. No shot, either.

T: Whatever you wish.
   (10-second interval.)

T: Anything?

A: Nothing.

T: Don't force, don't force. Let the thoughts come. Try to think of this grey man, what he looked like, what his name was, what he did, where did you see him most of the time, was he a friend, a relative, an uncle, perhaps –

A: Shut up, stop.
   (10-second interval.)

A: He's gone. I had him – I had him right on the brink – I almost remembered and now he's gone.
   (5-second interval.)

T: He'll return. The important thing is that you made contact. Remember earlier? How the clue of the dog led to the clue of Amy Hertz and that phone call. And the phone call led to the birth certificates –

A: I don't want to talk about all that. I want to go back to my room.

T: There is no hurry.

A: I'd prefer to go back.

T: Let us talk of something else.

A: I want to go to my room.
   (10-second interval.)

T: For instance, Paul Delmonte –

A: Is he the grey man?

T: Do you think he is?

A: I don't know. You asked me about him before. At the beginning. And I said I didn't want to talk about him. But I was bluffing. I didn't know who he was.

T: Do you know who is is now?

A: No.

T: Who do you think he is?

A: I want to go back. I'm not going to say another word.
   (5-second interval.)

T: As you wish. Let us suspend.

END TAPE OZK008

Robert Cormier

think
1 Which words and phrases convey a sense of fear in the extract?
2 What impression do you get of Adam and the psychoanalyst?
3 What is the setting of the first narrative? How do you imagine it differs from the second narrative?

choose
a *I am the Cheese* is told in a realistic setting in time and space; the fantasy element comes from the storyline and the way the plot is unfolded. Write your own fantasy thriller which takes place in a realistic setting.
b Part of the interest of the story comes from the switching between two different narrative styles. Write all or part of a story of your own, in which the story is told in more than one narrative style. This need not be a fantasy story.
c Assuming that the story continues in two narratives, predict what you think the ending will be, and give a full explanation of your decisions.
d How effective do you find the passage in terms of conveying a story and creating a sense of urgency? Write your own critique of the story saying what you do and do not find effective. You will need to think about the:

p163 ⟹

- characters,
- plot,
- style,
- narrative standpoint,
- setting.

The following two extracts come from *The Hitch Hiker's Guide to the Galaxy* by Douglas Adams, which is a comical science fiction fantasy. As you are reading them through, note the style of the writing and the way in which the passages are made comical. Look particularly at:

- the use of supposedly technical vocabulary;
- the balance of actual speech and explanation to the reader.

Mr L. Prosser was, as they say, only human. In other words he was a carbon-based bipedal life form descended from an ape. More specifically he was forty, fat and shabby and worked for the local council. Curiously enough, though he didn't know it, he was also a direct male-line descendant of Genghis Khan, though intervening generations and racial mixing had so juggled his genes that he had no discernible Mongoloid characteristics, and the only vestiges left in Mr L. Prosser of his mighty ancestry were a pronounced stoutness about the tum and a predilection for little fur hats.

He was by no means a great warrior: in fact he was a nervous worried man. Today he was particularly nervous and worried because something had gone seriously wrong with his job – which was to see that Arthur Dent's house got cleared out of the way before the day was out.

'Come off it, Mr Dent,' he said, 'you can't win you know. You can't lie in front of the bulldozer indefinitely.' He tried to make his eyes blaze fiercely but they just wouldn't do it.

Arthur lay in the mud and squelched at him.

'I'm game,' he said, 'we'll see who rusts first.'

'I'm afraid you're going to have to accept it,' said Mr Prosser gripping his fur hat and rolling it round the top of his head, 'this bypass has got to be built and it's going to be built!'

Mr Prosser said: 'You were quite entitled to make any suggestions or protests at the appropriate time you know.'

'Appropriate time?' hooted Arthur. 'Appropriate time? The first I knew about it was when a workman arrived at my home yesterday. I asked him if he'd come to clean the windows and he said no he'd come to demolish the house. He didn't tell me straight away of course. Oh no. First he wiped a couple of windows and charged me a fiver. Then he told me.'

'But Mr Dent, the plans have been available in the local planning office for the last nine months.'

'Oh yes, well as soon as I heard I went straight round to see them, yesterday afternoon. You hadn't exactly gone out of your way to call attention to them had you? I mean like actually telling anybody or anything.'

'But the plans were on display . . .'

'On display? I eventually had to go down to the cellar to find them.'

'That's the display department.'

'With a torch.'

'Ah, well the lights had probably gone.'

'So had the stairs.'

'But look, you found the notice didn't you?'

'Yes,' said Arthur, 'yes I did. It was on display in the bottom of a locked filing cabinet stuck in a disused lavatory with a sign on the door saying *Beware of the Leopard*.'

A cloud passed overhead. It cast a shadow over Arthur Dent as he lay propped up on his elbow in the cold mud. It cast a shadow over Arthur Dent's house. Mr Prosser frowned at it.

'It's not as if it's a particularly nice house,' he said.

'I'm sorry, but I happen to like it.'

'You'll like the bypass.'

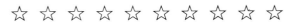

By a curious coincidence, *None at all* is exactly how much suspicion the ape-descendant Arthur Dent had that one of his closest friends was not descended from an ape, but was in fact from a small planet somewhere in the vicinity of Betelgeuse and not from Guildford as he usually claimed.

Arthur Dent had never, ever suspected this.

This friend of his had first arrived on the planet Earth some fifteen Earth years previously, and he had worked hard to blend himself into Earth society – with, it must be said, some success. For instance he had spent those fifteen years pretending to be an out of work actor, which was plausible enough.

He had made one careless blunder though, because he had skimped a bit on his preparatory research. The information he had gathered had led him to choose the name 'Ford Prefect' as being nicely inconspicuous.

He was not conspicuously tall, his features were striking but not conspicuously handsome. His hair was wiry and gingerish and brushed backwards from the temples. His skin seemed to be pulled backwards from the nose. There was something very slightly odd about him, but it was difficult to say what it was. Perhaps it was that his eyes didn't seem to blink often enough and when you talked to him for any length of time your eyes began involuntarily to water on his behalf. Perhaps it was that he smiled slightly too broadly and gave people the unnerving impression that he was about to go for their neck.

He struck most of the friends he had made on Earth as an eccentric, but a harmless one – an unruly boozer with some oddish habits. For instance he would often gatecrash university parties, get badly drunk and start making fun of any astrophysicists he could find till he got thrown out.

Sometimes he would get seized with oddly distracted moods and stare into the sky as if hypnotized until someone asked him what he was doing. Then he would start guiltily for a moment, relax and grin.

'Oh, just looking for flying saucers,' he would joke and everyone would laugh and ask him what sort of flying saucers he was looking for.

'Green ones!' he would reply with a wicked grin, laugh wildly for a moment and then suddenly lunge for the nearest bar and buy an enormous round of drinks.

Evenings like this usually ended badly. Ford would get out of his skull on whisky, huddle into a corner with some girl and explain to her in slurred phrases that honestly the colour of the flying saucers didn't matter that much really.

Thereafter, staggering semi-paralytic down the night streets he would often ask passing policemen if they knew the way to Betelgeuse. The policemen would usually say something like, 'Don't you think it's about time you went off home sir?'

'I'm trying to baby, I'm trying to,' is what Ford invariably replied on these occasions.

In fact what he was really looking for when he stared distractedly into the sky was any kind of flying saucer at all. The reason he said green was that green was the traditional space livery of the Betelgeuse trading scouts.

Ford Prefect was desperate that any flying saucer at all would arrive soon because fifteen years was a long time to get stranded anywhere, particularly somewhere as mindbogglingly dull as the Earth.

Ford wished that a flying saucer would arrive soon because he knew how to flag flying saucers down and get lifts from them. He knew how to see the Marvels of the Universe for less than thirty Altairian dollars a day.

In fact, Ford Prefect was a roving researcher for that wholly remarkable book *The Hitch Hiker's Guide to the Galaxy*.

Douglas Adams

think

1 Which elements in the story are typical of a science fiction story?
2 Select five words or phrases which you find particularly funny. What makes them humorous?
3 Douglas Adams makes the book more believable by beginning in a semi-real situation and then stretching the story beyond this. Pick out those ideas in the story which you find the most realistic.
4 When it was first published *The Hitch Hiker's Guide to the Galaxy* was extremely popular with teenage readers. What do you think the appeal may have been?

choose

a Describe one incident involving Arthur Dent and Ford Prefect which might occur later in the novel. *Either*:
   i) write the piece, as far as you can, in the comic style of the author,
   or:
   ii) carry out a piece of role play which allows the characters to meet and carry on the story.
b Rewrite the passage from *I Am the Cheese* in a comic style, taking note as you go of any parts which are difficult to alter.
c Write your own piece of comic fantasy. Try to make it as amusing and original as you can, don't simply imitate the style of *The Hitch Hiker's Guide to the Galaxy*.
d What makes this novel popular? Write your own close study of the passage, highlighting those features which would make it popular with a teenage readership. You could begin by carrying out a survey of the class to find out what they like or dislike about it.

105

2 Using fact for fiction

Below are two extracts from *The Thousand Eyes of Night* by Robert Swindells. Read them through carefully and then answer the questions which follow.

In this extract Simon, Diane and Tan are tied up and have been left in an old tunnel by the school bully, Deacon.

They fell to testing their bonds, and for a time nobody spoke. Presently, Tan broke the silence. 'My hands are a lot looser now,' he said. 'But I just can't loosen them enough to get free. What I need is somebody to have a go at the knots with his teeth, like they do in films sometimes. How about it, Simon?'

'Ugh!' Diane shivered. 'Bite that filthy flex? I wouldn't fancy it, Simon.' Tan glared at her.

'Would you rather stay here then?' he demanded. 'Or start screaming so that rat Deacon can kill himself laughing? Come on, Simon: give it a try.'

Simon, who was farthest from the entrance, made no reply. Tan peered at him in the gloom. 'Hey Simon, are you listening?' The boy had his back to the others and seemed to be staring into the blackness. After a moment he said, 'There's something in there. I can see something white.' He spoke in a dry whisper and Tan knew he was scared. He hoped he wasn't going to start making a noise, proving Deacon right.

'What is it?' he asked. 'That old ghost again? Maybe he'll have a go at this wire if we ask him nicely.' He chuckled, hoping to joke Simon out of his fear. It didn't work.

'It's white, and it's not moving, and I can see it better now,' whispered the frightened boy. Tan screwed up his eyes, peering in the same direction. There was something. He could see it himself. Up against the wall of the tunnel, maybe fifteen metres away. Something white, which didn't move. He swallowed hard.

'I see it,' he said, struggling to keep his voice even. 'It's probably a sheet of old

newspaper that's blown in. You can feel what a draught there is.' It was true. A steady stream of cold air flowed into the tunnel, carrying smoke from the fire outside. Where it went to he didn't know, because the other end was bricked up. Simon shook his head.

'It isn't paper,' he whispered. 'It's the wrong shape. I think it's a – I think it's . . .' His voice trailed off in a broken sob, and he began to struggle violently; thrashing about, making little noises in his throat like a wounded animal. Tan rolled, trying to get to his friend, hoping to calm him by being close.

There was no need. With a hoarse cry, Simon wrenched his hands free of the flex and began tearing at the knots which secured his ankles. He cursed and gibbered as he worked, hunched up over his knees; tugging and tearing and picking until, with a shout of triumph, he whipped away the flex and leapt to his feet.

Tan, sensing that his friend might run, yelled sharply. 'Simon! Here: help us.'

Simon glanced wildly into the darkness then knelt swiftly, picking at Tan's bonds with fumbling fingers. Tan felt the wire give, wrenched it slack with a kick and slipped his feet through. 'Get Diane!' he gasped. 'I'm off to look.'

He rolled over and got up, his hands still tied. He was scared, but his hatred of Deacon was stronger than his fear of whatever lay there in the dark. He could hear Diane behind him, encouraging her brother. He'd go right up to the thing and prove it harmless, and then the three of them would walk out into the light as though nothing had happened.

As he neared the object it began to assume a definite shape. He slowed, his scalp prickling. He took one pace. Two. He screwed up his eyes, his mouth dropped open and a wave of ice-cold dread washed over him. There, in the angle of floor and wall, lay the remains of a man.

Here Diane returns to the tunnel to find her satchel and is overcome by a hoard of 'mice' who think and move together.

The mouse scuttled into the tunnel and Diane followed, the satchel swinging and banging against her side. She was ten yards in before she realised what she was doing. She skidded to a stop. The mouse darted away into the gloom. Something brushed against her ankle and she flinched. A mouse ran past, followed at once by another. There came a sound like the patter of rain on dry leaves and a fast creamy foam swept out of the darkness like a wave racing in over sand. She turned, screaming, and began running back. The wave overtook her; became a live, furry carpet unrolling before her and she trod on soft, squealing lumps as she ran.

Out of the floor in front of her grew a soft white bulge. It grew outward and upward and became a thousand-eyed bear that loomed, gnashing its countless little teeth.

She screamed and tried to swerve round it but it knew, before she knew herself, the way that she would go. She started to turn. Something shifted under her shoe so that she fell and they swarmed on her, with their tiny, scampering feet and needle-teeth, and she knew that she would die. She began to shriek.

Through the echo of her screams, she heard her name. Somebody was calling: 'Diane. Diane.' The creatures ran over her face and entangled themselves in her hair. She swatted and clawed and cleared her mouth to cry, 'Here: I'm here!'

Rapid footfalls. Voices. Two silhouettes against the light, one of them wielding something, clubbing and slashing. Tan!

She managed to get up on her knees. The creatures began to let go: dropping from her body and darting away. She knelt in a sea of mice and plucked them off herself, sobbing. A woman came and lifted her to her feet and half-carried her towards the light. She recognised the reporter. They passed Tan, yelling and trampling, wielding a broken stake.

And then they were out in bright sunshine, running. The woman's arm circled Diane's waist and she ran awkwardly, half-sideways, supporting the girl. They climbed the slope, panting. Tan came last, looking back.

'Thank you,' gasped Diane, as the reporter helped her through the gap.

'Never mind that, love,' Liz Gordon replied. 'Here: lean on me.'

They hobbled towards the car.

Robert Swindells

In these extracts Swindells builds on realistic situations:
- a bully plays a trick on his victims:
- a girl goes to retrieve a satchel which she left in the tunnel earlier;

and on realistic emotions:

fear of:
- the dark,
- being tied up,
- being left alone,
- being bullied,
- being attacked,
- mice,

and makes the fears realities. He knows that his readers will be familiar with all of these fears, so he makes them just slightly worse by creating some extra variables, like mice who really are dangerous.

Use the following questions for discussion in preparation for the written work which follows.

1 Which part of the story do you find the most realistic?

2 Do you find the emotions of the characters realistic even if the situations are not? If you were in a tunnel with dangerous mice would you react in the same way Diane does?

3 Which aspect of the story do you find the most frightening?

4 What are your worst fears? Have any of them almost come true?

a Imagine another incident involving the mice, and write a continuation of the story.

b How did these terrifying animals come into being? Write the story before this story, of how the animals were created.

c Write your own fantasy fiction story which builds on common fears, and then makes them more horrific. Make your characters and setting as realistic as possible.

Read through the following story carefully and then answer the questions which follow. There is a break in the story just before the end to allow you to predict what happens.

Late Home

Where was she *this* time? It was always the same when he wanted to go out. Promises. Yes, I'll be back by then. And then he'd be waiting and looking at the clock and ringing the time and reading the small ads in the *Evening Telegraph* even though there was nothing he wanted – except to hear the car returning. As ever, his feelings were a mixture of annoyance and anxiety. What if . . . And anxiety heightened the annoyance because he was irritable at being made to worry, like the mother who scolds her child with the words 'Just think of all the worry you've caused us!' He looked down the road again. The conifer trees at the edge of the path were just visible. It had been dark for some time. Lights and engine noise awakened his spirits. It was the wrong noise: the car went straight past. How much traffic there was whenever you were waiting for someone! He noticed the coleus needed water. It always needed water but he couldn't bring himself to attend to it now. Waiting paralysed his ability to do anything else.

Another car passed. It was now very late. What a reputation he would be getting – remarks, half mocking, half serious, testing his patience even further. When she came he had every right to be angry, very angry. He need have no scruples about giving in to his annoyance this time.

She drove as swiftly as she dared. She was going to be a bit late and he would fuss and complain and probably go off in a bad mood and then all his friends, or colleagues as he called them, would think he was a fool to put up with her – and that she was unreliable and, of course, just like a woman! So what? But she drove a little faster, turning off the heater and opening the window. The stream of brisk evening air disturbed her twenty-five pound hair style but again she thought, so what? The black strands wisped in front of her eyes.

The road narrowed and curved. On either side were high, unkempt hawthorn hedges and behind them the remains of old chalk quarries: large white sores that wouldn't heal. Headlights swept towards her. She kept her hands steady and her eyes rigidly on the air just to the left of the lights. At such times she always felt that she had become invisible to the other driver, who would only realise her existence after the impact. The lorry swept past: a gust of hot air and diesel fumes and total unconcern.

The car headlamps picked out figures in the road ahead. There seemed to be two or three people, making no attempt to keep in to the side of the road. She slowed, trying to make out what they were doing. If they didn't move, she was going to hit one of them, the fools . . . She was about to press the horn button when she saw that one of the figures, a man, dressed in a white T-shirt and dark trousers, was signalling her to stop. She hesitated between panic and calm, between pressing the accelerator and pressing the brake. She stopped, uncertainly but with irritation. She

didn't have time to give lifts to people.

They all looked much the same: light coloured T-shirts with faded emblems and slogans, dark jeans, pale unshaven faces. The first one put his right hand on the window sill of the car and his other hand on the roof. A position of ease and familiarity. He leant down, his head almost through the open window.

'Sorry to stop you. I wonder if you can help us?'

She noticed two drops of sweat on his upper lip. She wanted him to wipe them away, irritated with his presumption and with the delay.

'Yes?' she said, coolly, reservedly, in a manner which suited her high necked white blouse with the delicate stitching.

'There's someone here who needs to get to the hospital.'

She glanced around. She could only see one person behind him, just the right half of a person in fact – a right half that looked perfectly healthy. Thoughts ran rapidly: there was no one ill or injured – yes there was – she would have to – but he had a dreadful disease, infectious, horrid – he was bleeding – he would die in the car . . .

'I'm already late . . .' she started to say, not forcefully enough. Why weren't there any other cars? Where was the traffic, where the headlights glaring?

'He needs to get to the hospital.' The manner of the statement brought back her annoyance. It was assertive, it assumed a right to travel in her car, her clean car. She was about to say, in her most effective, haughty tone, 'Very well then, I'll telephone for an ambulance at the next call-box,' when she noticed two things almost simultaneously. The third man was at the other side of the car, his hand on the side of the car, his hand on the door handle. The second man had come closer. Her pulse jumped. He was carrying a long bladed knife, like a pruning tool. She thought, but did not say, 'Help'. Her left hand put the car into gear, her right hand tightened on the

109

steering wheel. The man who had been speaking to her started to open her door – indeed, he had both hands round the top of the door frame. A vision of the men climbing into the car on each side of her, crushing her between them, seized her. Without thought and seemingly without effort, she pulled on the door with her right hand, gripped the wheel with her left, pushed down with her right foot and took her left off the clutch. The car leapt forward, roaring.

Then confusion took over. Was she screaming or wasn't she? Had she got away or were they with her somehow? Why was it so awfully noisy? Oncoming lights focussed a part of her mind. She thought of steering, thought of slowing down, realised the car was doing nearly twenty miles an hour in first gear, forced herself to stare ahead, not in the mirror, forced herself to change gear. I'm safe: I've got away. Fear changed into a strange exultation, a sort of childish excitement. She moved into top gear and raced on down the road, turned onto the dual carriageway with a Hollywood screech and kept her foot obstinately on the accelerator pedal.

She had travelled several miles before she recollected that she was not on the right road home. By the time she had found a roundabout other reactions had begun. I'm trembling, she thought. They say that's what happens. It's shock. You tremble. I must stop. I might have an accident.

He sighed. It was a sigh of worry rather than annoyance now. Then he thought things through logically. If she had left at such a time, taken so long to drive, then it would be . . . and she wasn't all that late, not late enough to signal an accident or a breakdown – just late enough for someone who didn't take enough care about punctuality, who could never say goodbye to anyone, who valued her time more than his. If only her money hadn't paid for half the car – more than half the car! Had he smoked, he would have been lighting cigarette

after cigarette now. Instead, he adjusted his tie, combed his hair, ran his fingers through his hair, combed it again, sighed, kicked the plant pot, scraped the polish on his shoe and swore. He brushed at the mark on the leather half-heartedly. The telephone rang.

As he was walking towards the phone, trying not to run, he heard a car – their car. He answered the phone: the second wrong number that evening. The car came up the short drive and stopped alongside the porch. He marched righteously outside. She leant over from the driver's side to greet him, smiling weakly he thought. She slid over to the passenger side, opened the door and was only half out when he spoke.

'Where have you been? Do you know what time it is?'

She said nothing. Her stomach contracted. He would never believe her. How could she say it all? What *had* happened?

'I was stopped . . .' she began, and took a breath. How could she find the words to say it all?

'Stopped? You're always being made to stop by someone. It's impossible – trying to keep arrangements with you. You have no idea . . .'

She stood by the doorway. He was half in the still open car-door. She wanted to cry but she wouldn't: she suddenly hated him because he didn't care. She wouldn't tell him, then he'd be in the wrong and she'd be in the right.

'I've been worrying – thinking you've had an accident: broken down in some dark street . . . and you were just taking your time, driving along with the radio on and wondering what excuse to use this time!'

Her resolution to say nothing gave way. 'I was stopped by some men,' she said again. She could smell her own sweat, though the white blouse looked as crisp as ever.

'A good one!' he said, half turning away. 'What did they do, jump out of the telegraph wires on to the roof of the car? Batter their way in through the windscreen?' Pleased with his humour, he slammed the door, slid across to the steering wheel and started to drive away. When he glanced in the mirror she was no longer at the door. Gone in to comb her hair already, he thought, well, tonight I won't worry about being late home.

Inside the house she was in the bathroom, being sick. Reaction, she thought. Shock. But I didn't scream; I just drove away. Yet I remember the sound of screaming.

> Now write the ending to the story, in rough. Having written some ideas down, read the ending on the next page. How closely did your ideas match up? Which ending do you prefer?

think

1 Pick out any aspects of the story which seem to be
- completely believable;
- likely to be true;
- unlikely to be true;
- unbelievable.

2 Why do you think the writer uses two voices in the story?

3 Select those words and phrases which you find the most effective in terms of:
- generating fear;
- creating suspense;
- describing a scene accurately;

and state the reasons for your choice.

choose

a Write the sequel to the story. What happens when the man discovers what it is he has found? Keep the two dialogues (man and woman) to describe what happens next.

p163

b Write a review of the story *Late Home*, stating what you find effective in the piece. How good is it as a short story? In what ways does it use reality to create fantasy?

c Rewrite the story to make it slightly more of a fantasy. You should think of some more fantastical events which might occur, or simply explain the events which have happened in a different way.

111

He arrived at the club, now merely cross in a cold way, a way that wouldn't forgive and forget easily. The car parking attendant came to open the door. As he stepped out, he felt something touch him. Something fell to the ground that had been trapped in the door jamb. Without thinking, he bent and picked it up. It was a greyish brown, long and thin. At first he thought it was a vegetable of some sort. Then, with the attendant staring at him, he realised what he held: it was a human finger, wrenched off at the joint.

Trevor Millum

d   The following is a factual account of an incident which took place at Borley Rectory. Read it through carefully and then use it as the basis for your own fantasy story. You can introduce any characters you wish into the story but you must include the narrator, and the actual setting described.

At 10.30 p.m. I leaned my bicycle against the stone wall of the churchyard, and stood for a few moments, looking up the path towards the porch and door. I could just see the dusty white of the gravel path, the dim blurred outlines of the yew trees that bordered it, and the shape of the gabled porch. The people retire to bed early in the country, and I saw not a soul; I went in crêpe-soled shoes to the porch and sat down upon a seat and began my vigil. Presently a crescent moon gave just enough light for me to see objects fairly clearly. Several times I looked at my watch. A few nesting birds rustled in the trees and the creeper that clothed the wall of the house adjoining the churchyard. There was the occasional lowing of cattle in the meadows near the river, and the hoot of an owl somewhere in the distance. That was all – in between the sounds there was complete silence.

It was a warm summer night – there was no breath of wind. I looked at my watch; it was 11.43 p.m. Then I think I must have dozed. I jerked awake – because I had heard the latch on the churchyard gate click. The time was 12.16 a.m.

I do not think I was actually afraid, but I was aware of a certain amount of fear: the doubting sensation with which one probes the unknown, the caution with which one accepts a bargain from a stranger. Then I heard steps coming up the path. They paused for a second near one of the yew bushes. The light was clear. The footsteps continued but there was no one near. I sensed someone passing me, there was a chillness in the air and I felt a slight pressure. Whatever it was I knew and felt that it was essentially EVIL. I also knew that I resented in some way hearing and not seeing. I then heard the sound of a key in the lock, then the creak of the door hinges as the door opened. I heard the door close. A few seconds later I heard soft notes and chords from the organ. The time was 12.18.

extra   Going beyond

Some of our fantasies could be realities, if the reports of witnesses are to be believed. Below is an eye-witness account describing the sighting of an unidentified flying object (UFO). Read it through carefully and then answer the questions which follow.

'Humanoids . . . and strange insignia'

At about 5.50 p.m. on 24 April 1964 Patrolman Lonnie Zamora of the Police Department in Socorro, New Mexico, was alone in his Pontiac giving chase to a speeding motorist who was heading out of town. Suddenly he heard a roar and at the same time saw a 'flame' in the sky, bluish and orange and strangely static as it descended some distance away. Fearful that a nearby dynamite shack might blow up, the patrolman gave up chasing the motorist and headed off over rough ground towards the point where the flame had come down.

After three attempts he forced his car to the top of a ridge and drove slowly

westwards. He stopped when, suddenly, he saw a shiny, aluminium-like object below him, about 150–200 yards (140–185 metres) south of his position. Zamora said it looked like a car on end, perhaps 'turned over by some kids'. Then he saw two humanoid figures in white 'coveralls' close to the object. He estimated later that they were about 4 feet (1.2 metres) tall. One of them looked straight at him and seemed to jump. Zamora was wearing clip-on sunglasses over his prescription spectacles and couldn't distinguish any features or headgear at that distance.

The patrolman now accelerated thinking that, whoever the strangers were, they might be in need of help. The shape he'd seen was a sort of vertical oval, and looking down he could see it was supported on girderlike legs. When the terrain became too rough for the car to go any further he radioed his headquarters to say that he was near the scene of a possible accident and would proceed on foot.

As Zamora left the car he heard two or three loud thumps, like someone hammering or slamming a door. These thumps were a second or two apart. When he was about 50 paces from the object there was a loud roar, which rose gradually in pitch. The humanoid figures were nowhere to be seen. At the same time he could see a blue and orange flame rise from the ground leaving a cloud of dust. Zamora beat a hasty retreat towards his car and as he reached it turned to see the oval shape, now horizontal, rising towards the level of the car. Frightened by the continuing roar, he ran on and dived for shelter over the edge of the ridge. When he realised the noise had ceased he raised his head from his hands and saw the UFO still in the air and moving away from him about 15 feet (4.5 metres) above the ground. It safely cleared the dynamite shack and continued to rise gradually, watched by the policeman, who was retracing his steps to the car. As he called up the radio

officer he watched it accelerate away to clear a mountain range and disappear.

Zamora had seen a kind of strange insignia about 18 inches (45 centimetres) high on the side of the object and while he was waiting for his sergeant to arrive he decided to make a sketch of it.

Sergeant Sam Chavez was soon on the scene. Had he not taken a wrong turning he would have arrived in time to see the craft.

'What's the matter, Lonnie?' he asked. 'You look like you've seen the devil.'

'Maybe I have,' replied Zamora.

Zamora pointed out to Seargeant Chavez the fire that was still burning in the bush where the UFO had stood. When they descended to the site they found four separate burn marks and four depressions – all of similar shape – made, they assumed, by the legs of the landing gear. On three of the marks the dense soil had been pushed down about 2 inches (50 millimetres) and dirt had been squeezed up at the sides. The fourth pad mark, less well defined, was only 1 inch (25 millimetres) deep. When engineer W.T. Powers investigated the case he estimated that the force that produced the marks was 'equivalent to a gentle settling of at least a ton on each mark.' He also pointed out an interesting fact about the positions of the marks. Measurements show that the diagonals of a quadrilateral intersect at right angles, then the midpoints of the sides all lie on the circumference of a circle. Mr Powers noted that one of the burn marks occurred on the intersection of the diagonals and speculated that, assuming the linkage among the legs was flexible, this would mean the burn was immediately below the centre of gravity of the craft and might indicate the position of the blue and orange flame seen by Patrolman Zamora. Four small round marks were found within the quadrilateral on the side farthest from where Patrolman Zamora had stood; these were described as 'footprints'.

The Socorro incident was widely reported in the press and generated immense excitement throughout the world. The US Air Force's Project Blue Book usually ruled out UFO sightings with only one witness, but at Socorro Patrolman Zamora's story was so plausible that it was decided to carry out intensive on-the-spot investigations. This was one case in which Project Blue Book was forced to admit defeat: the apparition could not be explained as any known device or phenomenon. Dr J. Allen Hynek admitted that he was more puzzled after completing the investigation than when he had arrived in Socorro. He commented, 'Maybe there *is* a simple natural explanation for the Socorro incident, but having made a complete study of the events, I do not think so.'

think

1 Pick out those words and phrases which tell you the witness's attitude to what he saw.

2 Write a brief character sketch of the witness. Would you expect him to be reliable?

choose

p175

a You are a reporter who has an opportunity to interview the witness. Carry out a role play of the interview, and then write it up as a front page news story.

b How many people in your class believe in UFO's? What do they think they are like? Carry out a survey, or a series of interviews, to glean information from your classmates. Then report your findings to the group.

c Carry out some research into another unexplained phenomenon (e.g. the Loch Ness monster, the Yeti, how Stonehenge was built). Write up your findings in a full report.

d Write a piece of creative writing called 'The Sighting'.

starter   **Bob Geldof**

In 1984 a famine in Ethiopia was reported on the BBC News in a brief, but very graphic video, which showed the starving people queueing for food in their thousands. The public reaction was enormous, and led to several fund raising appeals, and pressure on the British government to send famine relief.

Bob Geldof, the driving force behind Band Aid and Live Aid, has written a book about these fund raising events and the Ethiopian famine which prompted them. In the extract below he describes how he saw this as a personal response to the tragedy.

Is That It?

It was coming to the end of 1984 and I could see no prospect for the release of an album the Boomtown Rats and I had sweated over and were proud of. All day I had been on the phone trying to promote a single from the album. I went home in a state of blank resignation and switched on the television. But there I saw something that placed my worries in a ghastly new perspective.

The news report was of famine in Ethiopia. From the first seconds it was clear that this was a horror on a monumental scale. The pictures were of people who were so shrunken by starvation that they looked like beings from another planet. Their arms and legs were as thin sticks, their bodies spindly. Swollen veins and huge, blankly staring eyes protruded from their shrivelled heads. The camera wandered amid them like a mesmerised observer, occasionally dwelling on one person so that he looked directly at me, sitting in my comfortable living room. And there were children, their bodies fragile and vulnerable as premature babies but with the consciousness of what is happening to them gleaming dully from their eyes. All around was the murmur of death like a hoarse whisper, or the buzzing of flies.

From the first few seconds it was clear that this was a tragedy which the world had somehow contrived not to notice until it had reached a scale which constituted an international scandal. You could hear that in the tones of reporter Michael Buerk. It was the voice of a man who was registering despair, grief and disgust at what he was seeing. At the end the newscasters remained silent. Paula burst into tears, and then rushed upstairs to check on our baby, Fifi, who was sleeping peacefully in her cot.

The images played and replayed in my mind. What could I do? Did not the sheer scale of the thing call for something more? Michael Buerk had used the word biblical: a famine of biblical proportions.

A horror like this could not occur today without our consent. We had allowed this to happen. I would send money. But that was not enough. I was stood against the wall. I had to withdraw my consent. What else could I do? I was only a pop singer – and by now not a very successful pop singer. All I could do was make records that no one bought. But I would do that, I would give the profits of the next Rats record to Oxfam. What good would that do? It would be a pitiful amount. But it would be more than I could raise by simply dipping into my shrunken bank account. Maybe some people would buy it just because the profits were going to Oxfam. And I would withdraw my consent. Yet that was not enough.

Bob Geldof

1 What aspects of the famine did Bob Geldof find the most horrifying as he thought about the news report he had just seen?

2 Why do you think the camera is described as a 'mesmerised observer'? What is meant by this?

3 Put into your own words the phrase: 'a tragedy which the world had somehow contrived not to notice'.

4 Why do you think he saw the need for a personal response?

5 Why do you think so many people donate money to charities?

a From the account above and the accompanying picture, give your own 'gut' reactions to the famine. Present these as a story, a report, or a poem.

b Not everyone could have organized Band Aid, Live Aid or the events which followed. It took an exceptional individual in the person of Bob Geldof. Organize a small group discussion to highlight the particular character traits necessary to start up and coordinate such a venture.

p169

c Carry out some research into the Ethiopian famine of 1984, or into any other disaster, which has previously, or is currently, hitting the headlines. Prepare a factual account, giving information about the event, which you can present to the class.

p156

d Some people have accused those rock stars who took part in Band Aid of jumping on the bandwagon in order to promote their own careers. Write a letter, which one of the music personalities might have written, to respond to this accusation.

1

Alone

The Lonely Ladies of Manhattan

The lonely ladies of Manhattan hurry down the sidewalks purposefully, frowning as if there is something more definite ahead than being alone a bit longer.

'You *can't* just wander. You stop to look around you and there's always some joker waiting for you. Either it's just another pick up . . . Or it's just a nut. There was this girl in the next apartment to me. She was crazy. She was fresh to New York from some hick place in Pennsylvania and she kept saying, "Oh this excitement in the air, oh this hint of danger." Oh she found it so stimulating. So one night she gets stabbed on East 55th at around 3.35 am. Now me, I would never hang around East 55th or anywhere else at 3.35 am. Not while I want to stay healthy.'

As for eating; 'You know the best places to eat, the very best on your own? Kennedy Airport, that's where. Just after I quit that snake in the grass of a husband of mine that's what I used to do, take the bus out to Kennedy. Well I know I was crazy then, I really was. It's like this. You get a nice class of people to talk to, nobody bothers you. You got a reason for being there. I don't go out there anymore. Well I guess I've kind of got used to things a bit. Well perhaps I should say there's this neighbourhood place I can go to. Italian. I figured it this way, by going to the same place, there was a chance I'd meet someone.

'Oh I've tried the clubs and the agencies. I've had all that. Look, you go to a Friendship Club, what do you get? A lot of jerks that's what. You get some unfunny things happening at Friendship Clubs. There was this one I went to. It was a sort of party at somebody's apartment. The organizer's I guess. You paid 10 dollars. For 10 dollars you got a glass of wine and a number. After a half hour this organizer says, "Boys and girls lets take a role call." He calls out the numbers. That's how you're paired off. It's automatic. No will you, won't you. The lights go out and they all get on with it. I don't want just that. I'm looking for relationships.'

The ones who look the loneliest have a touching Dorothy Parker[1]ish tinge to them. Lipstick too bright and very slightly off course; they wear veils and/or bows and there is a hollow glint of too much crying in their eyes. When you talk to them they all start off on the same sort of brave front, the chat about 'my career', 'my social life', but it breaks down terrifyingly soon. 'I was saying to my friends, the McWhirters, at their cocktail last night, he's a writer, she's a very talented artist, I said "Look darlings I can't come to you for dinner again because I'm already promised" . . . 'and five minutes later her voice slows down: "What I can't understand is how anyone gets to know *anyone* in New York City. Anyone O.K. that is. I look at people when the lights go up at the movies and I think, well how do you do it, how do you get together like that. Because I know not everyone is a jerk or a pick up." '

Pauline Peters

[1] *Dorothy Parker was a fashionable American writer in the 1930s.*

think

1 Select some words and phrases in the passage which tell the reader where it is set.
2 Why do you think the woman tells the interviewer about the invitations she has turned down?
3 Put into your own words the reasons why the woman went to Kennedy Airport.
4 Pauline Peters has formed statements about loneliness from a series of interviews in Manhattan. Looking back through the passage, write down what her ten main interview questions might have been.

choose

p169

a Write an exchange of letters which might have been written between two lonely ladies in Manhattan.
b Using your list of questions (adapted if necessary), hold interviews with the members of your class on the subject of loneliness, consider who in society is likely to be lonely and whether some occupations cause loneliness.
c Write an essay entitled 'Alone'.
d Sometimes being alone is a pleasurable activity. Look at the following pictures and discuss them with a partner. Then complete one of the assignments which follow.

p175

i) Using the pictures above as an initial idea, write a story about a person on her/his own.
ii) Prepare a talk on the advantages of doing something alone. Allow your ideas to be stimulated by the pictures above.
iii) Lonely or alone? Write a story or poem in which someone on her/his own becomes lonely, or a lonely person comes to enjoy her/his aloneness.

Some jobs make life very lonely for people. George Wood was born in 1914 and spent most of his life working in hospital jobs. He wrote this report whilst working at Hackney hospital in the 1970s. In 1976 he was admitted to hospital himself and died there.

Mortuary Technician

I have got to know the local undertakers pretty well over the years. You do get one from out of town occasionally and you don't know him: they come from Scotland, up north or Wales. They'll phone and say, 'Can I pick up the body at such-and-such a time?' and I'll say, 'Yeah of course,' and maybe stay open late for them. Or they'll come overnight and say, 'Can we pick it up in the morning. We're coming from Wales, Scotland or whatever.' But normally, 99 times out of 100, they're people I know, from round the area.

I have only had one misunderstanding with an undertaker. People ask whether bodies get mixed up. Well it can happen. It shouldn't, but where the human element comes in, it can happen. It happened to me once. An undertaker came and took the wrong body. We were busy in the Post Mortem room at the time. It was my fault for not checking and it was his fault for not checking. I just said, 'That's the one'; he took it and it was the wrong body. After a while we found out. There was quite a kerfuffle. We phoned the undertaker and he said, 'Oh, it's in my chapel,' which was fortunate. If it had been a cremation, it would have been taken straight to the cemetary and we wouldn't have got it back. There would have been an awful stink then of course. As it was, it was a burial. These things do happen. They shouldn't but they do. It's happened to me now, once. That's the only case I can remember. I do check that the undertaker takes the right body if possible, but if you're busy in the Post Mortem room and an undertaker knocks on the door, you go, 'Help yourself, like.' You shouldn't but you do . . .

I've been at it thirty years. It suits me, this job. There are no guv'nors breathing down my neck. Certain things have to be done, so I do them; but nobody tells me to. I used to come under the Head Porter, but now I'm under the Path. Lab.

After work I forget about it. I might think 'I'll go in a bit earlier tomorrow' if I've got a Post Mortem first thing, but I don't take the work home with me (metaphorically speaking, of course!). Once I've finished, I've finished. Most people who do this work tend to live with it all the time. They're married to it; it's their whole life. But not me. To me it's just a means to an end. I get money on a Friday, which is all I'm interested in.

George Wood

1 What would you like or dislike about George's job in the mortuary?
2 Put into your own words exactly what happened when the body went missing.
3 What does George mean when he says: 'I don't take the work home with me (metaphorically speaking of course!).'?

a Imagine you are one of the people involved in the incident when the body gets lost. You could be a relative, the undertaker, or another hospital worker. Write a playscript of the drama. The script can be comic or serious.

p161 ▷ **b** What does George see as the good and bad points of the job he does? Start by writing down a list of points and then write this up as an informative piece of writing. You can *report* but you should not *quote* George's speech.

c   George says: 'I get money on Friday which is all I'm interested in'. Which do you think is more important, enjoying your work or being paid well for it? Write an imaginary debate between two characters, one of whom thinks enjoyment is more important, the other, money.

d   Think of another job which might lead to loneliness. Write a diary for a day doing this job.

2 Individuality

Some people simply stand out from a crowd; there is something about them that catches the eye or intrigues. They have individuality.

Read through the poem below and then answer the questions which follow it:

Living off other people – Welfare

It would be pretty to have roses
Flourishing by my back door.
It would be nice to have a well-kept house
With velvet chairs not scraping a polished floor.
It would be lovely to sit down at dinner
Grey tie, pearl pin, fresh shirt and well-kept hands
And good to have a purring car in a clean garage
Eye-catching as the best brass bands.

But to keep it all going would be a lot of worry
And anyone who does it has to race and scurry
Seeing to roofs and pruning, maintenance and mechanics,
A shower of rain, a little green fly, bring on terrible panics
And ruin and failure shadow every path.

So I think this is the best thing to do:
As I walk down roads I see so many flowers
Nod-nodding in all the gardens that I pass.
I can glance into other people's rooms that they have furnished
And look how courteously that man is turning
To open the front door to his gleaming house.
Did you see how his suit fitted him, his perfect cuffs? Spotless cars
Slide by the women in furs and perfumes
Wafted to me with the flavour of cigars.

I am wrapped in my layers of shapeless coats
And I need never polish or dig or set
The table out for our distinguished guests
Or get to an office or prove myself each day
To provide for hammocks and lawns.
To get my antiques protected against insects.
A guest everywhere, I look in as dinner is served.
As I tramp past others' gardens, the rose opens.

(from Beyond Descartes)   *Jenny Joseph*

121

think
1 Make a list of the things which the person in the poem would like to have.
2 In what ways are her/his needs met by a life on the road?

choose
a Why do you think the poem is called 'Living off other people – Welfare'? Give reasons and then think of some alternative titles for the poem explaining why you think they are appropriate.
b In this poem the writer creates a positive image of poverty. Write your own poem or description which shows the negative side.
c Rehearse a discussion between two vagrants saying what they like and dislike about their lives.
d Write a description of a person you know whose appearance and actions make them distinctive.

Below are two extracts which describe individuals in great detail. In both cases the person being described is an attractive woman. Read the pieces through carefully.

The Great Gatsby

A breeze blew through the room, blew curtains in at one end and out at the other like pale flags, twisting them up towards the frosted wedding-cake of the ceiling, and then rippled over the wine-coloured rug, making a shadow on it as wind does on the sea.

The only completely stationary object in the room was an enormous couch on which two young women were buoyed up as though upon an anchored balloon. They were both in white, and their dresses were rippling and fluttering as if they had just been blown back after a short flight around the house. I must have stood for a few moments listening to the whip and snap of the curtains and the groan of a picture on the wall. Then there was a boom as Tom Buchanan shut the rear windows and the caught wind died out about the room, and the curtains and the rugs and the two young women ballooned slowly to the floor.

The younger of the two was a stranger to me. She was extended full length at her end of the divan, completely motionless, and with her chin raised a little, as if she were balancing something on it which was quite likely to fall. If she saw me out of the corner of her eyes she gave no hint of it, indeed I was almost surprised into murmuring an apology for having disturbed her by coming in.

The other girl, Daisy, made an attempt to rise, she leaned slightly forward with a conscientious expression(1), then she laughed, an absurd(2), charming little laugh, and I laughed too and came forward into the room,
'I'm p-paralysed with happiness.'
She laughed again, as if she said something very witty, and held my hand for a moment, looking up into my face, promising that there was no one in the world she so much wanted to see. That was a way she had. She hinted in a murmur that the surname of the balancing girl was Baker. (I've heard it said that Daisy's murmur was only to make people lean toward her; an irrelevant (3) criticism that made it no less charming.)

F. Scott Fitzgerald

1. deliberate seriousness
2. inappropriate, silly
3. unimportant

122

The French Lieutenant's Woman

She turned and sat quickly and gracefully sideways on a hammock several feet in front of the tree, so that she turned and faced the sea: and so, as Charles found when he took the better seat, that her face was half hidden from him – and yet again, by some ingenious coquetry(1), so that he must take note of her hair. She sat very upright, yet with head bowed, occupied in an implausible(2) adjustment of her bonnet. Charles watched her, with a smile in his mind if not on his lips. He could see she was at a loss how to begin: and yet the situation was too *al fresco*(3), too informally youthful, as if they were a boy and sister, for the shy formality she betrayed.

She put the bonnet aside, and loosened her coat, and sat with her hands folded; but still she did not speak. Something about the coat's high collar and cut, especially from the back, was masculine – it gave her a touch of the air of a girl coachman, a female soldier – a touch only, and which the hair effortlessly contradicted. With a kind of surprise Charles noticed how shabby clothes did not detract from her; in some way they even suited her, and more than finer clothes might have done. The last five years had seen a great emancipation(4) in women's fashions, at least in London. The first artificial aids to a well shaped bosom had begun to commonly be worn; eyelashes and eyebrows were painted, lips salved, hair 'dusted' and tinted . . . and by most fashionable women, not just those of the *demi-monde*(5). Now with Sarah there was none of this. She seemed totally indifferent to fashion; and survived in spite of it, just as the simple primroses at Charles' feet survived all the competition of exotic conservatory plants.

John Fowles

> 1. clever flirting   2. unlikely
> 3. in the open air/informal
> 4. greater freedom less limitation   5. the fashion-conscious rich

think

1. Pick out those words and phrases which suggest that the woman in each passage is beautiful.
2. Pick out those words and phrases which suggest that Daisy and Sarah are manipulating other people.
3. Describe those qualities which are seen to be unique to Daisy.
4. In what ways are Daisy and Sarah similar?
5. In what ways is the setting used to make the women seem more attractive?

choose

a From the factual information given in the passage build up a profile of either Daisy or Sarah. Once the facts are established, add to the profile information which is likely to be true, but is not necessarily so.

p154 **b** Write your own description of someone, so that the reader will find them attractive. Use the techniques Fitzgerald and Fowles employ, of placing the person in a beautiful setting, and making them appear a little mysterious. You can *either* write as if you are involved in the scene (*The Great Gatsby*) *or* as if you are observing from the outside (*The French Lieutenant's Woman*).

c Imagine a mysterious, but rather attractive person visiting your school. Begin by describing them, and then tell the story of their visit and how they are received.

p154 **d** The poem 'Living off other people – Welfare' and the extracts from the two novels give close descriptions of people who are eccentric and attractive. Write a close description of someone you find interesting.

3

Against society

People are set against society for many different reasons. The first extract shows how a person's political beliefs can isolate them from important aspects of society, and in a later extract from *It's My Life* we see how Jan is isolated because of a change in her social circumstances. Sometimes a person chooses to separate from society, and sometimes it is not a matter of choice.

The following extracts are taken from a play by Tom Stoppard called *Squaring the Circle*. It concerns the growth and defeat of the Solidarity movement in Poland. Solidarity, an illegal union, fought for the rights of workers, but was crushed by the existing Government, leading eventually to martial law in Poland.

Between August 1980 and December 1981 an attempt was made in Poland to put together two ideas which wouldn't fit, the idea of freedom as it is understood in the West, and the idea of socialism as it is understood in the Soviet empire. The attempt failed because it was impossible, in the same sense as it is impossible in geometry to turn a circle into a square with the same area – not because no one has found out how to do it, but because there is no way in which it can be done. What happened in Poland was that a number of people tried for sixteen months to change the shape of the system without changing the area covered by the original shape. They failed.

Parliament. Day.
Jaruzelski is at the microphone.

Jaruzelski: In the Central Committee, even in the Politburo, there are voices asking us to set our democratic system aside until peace is restored. What I will ask of this assembly is to prepare itself for a situation where I will have to come to you and ask for emergency laws. There are 12,000 on strike in the textile mills. If the independent union cannot control its anarchists, we will have to find some other way . . .

. . . Government Meeting Room. Day.
On one side of the large table is Rakowski *flanked by two advisors. He is faced by* Walesa *similarly attended.*

Walesa: I was in the textile mills. I have met these anarchists . . . 12,000 women, young girls and grannies, working wives . . . Do you think they're on strike because they want to overthrow the Party? No, they're on strike because work brings no reward, and it doesn't look as if the Government knows what to do about it. They get up in the dark to stand in line for hours to buy a pair of shoes the wrong size so that they may have something to barter for a piece of meat – which turns out to be rotten. They appeal to you and you say – oh, we can't help it, these anarchists are making life impossible. And then it turns out *they're* the anarchists! Listen, they can't break the circle, someone else has to. I don't think you can do it on your own.

Rakowski: I agree. You know our proposal – an action front representing all the social forces – the Government, Solidarity, the Church, the peasants, the official unions, Catholic intellectuals, economists, scientists – a team of national unity –

Walesa: You just want to water us down. But we're 10 million and we won't sit down as equal partners with the incompetents and the hacks – the central planners, the time-savers, the seat warmers – all the ones who had the chance and lost it. You've failed, and the best answer now is an economic council, independent, with real power, made up of Solidarity and Government equally with equal voices.

Rakowski: *(Angrily)* What sort of Government do you expect to hand over its authority to a committee?

Walesa: Your sort. A government with no mandate at the end of its string.

*(*Rakowski *insulted, gets up from the table and walks away, perhaps towards a window. His advisers look stonily across the table.* Walesa *and the* Solidarity men *stand up and prepare to leave.)*

Rakowski: Perhaps you'd better tell that to the General?

Walesa: *(with conscious irony)* Do you mean the Prime Minister?

Rakowski: Yes, the Prime Minister. The First Secretary. The General.

Walesa: How many votes does he get?

Tom Stoppard

think

1 How does Jaruzelski's view of the 'anarchists' in the factories differ from Walesa's view?

2 What is the difference between the 'team of National unity' proposed by Rakowski an[d] the 'economic council' proposed by Walesa?

3 Talk about and write down some brief notes on how the play portrays Jaruzelski, Walesa and Rakowski.

4 Put into your own words the meaning Stoppard gives to the phrase 'squaring the circle'.

5 What do you think is meant by 'they can't break the circle, someone else has to.'?

choose

a Write a report on your impressions of Walesa.

b Walesa and Solidarity were eventually isolated from society because of their beliefs. Find out about any individual in the past or present, who has been isolated because of their political beliefs. The pictures below may give you some ideas. Present your findings in an illustrated project.

c Imagine yourself as an individual whose ideas differ from the politics of the day. Write [a] short story explaining your beliefs and what happens to you as a result of them. You should attempt to make the story sound true, even though it is fictitious.

Nelson Mandela

Martin Luther King

As well as having to cope with the emotional trauma of her mother leaving home, Jan is faced with two other difficulties; she has to take over the running of the house, and face the attitudes of others. The following extract highlights the stigma which is attached to the fact that her mother has left home.

It's My Life

The next day as she bent over her desk, she saw the face of Miss Maudesley, her tutor, eyes anxious behind large glasses, close to her own, asking some questions she could not quite catch. But she answered.

'I'm quite all right thank you.'

She must have spoken loudly for several of her classmates turned and stared. Miss Maudesley walked away as though offended. Jan knew she ought to say something, to put things right. But the heaviness in her held her back. Only by the greatest strength of will did she go from day to day, and each word she must speak to others was a burden.

She had gone into a tunnel with no end in sight and no view to left or right – school, home, shops, kitchen, stairs, bedroom, books, work, sleep. She moved so from day to day, from place to place, and did not know how she reached each point in her familiar round. She saw people but did not look at them, spoke to them, but did not hear what they said. Nothing was real and nothing could be felt, but the heavy ache deep inside her.

On the fourth day, she found herself in the early evening with women from the works, picking up bits and pieces in the supermarket. The cash lady was thin and sharp-nosed with china-blue eyes and a Mrs Thatcher hairdo. Every six months the supermarket changed hands and she swapped overalls, bright green, dark blue, candy stripe. But she was always there, dipping her head like a sparrow, exchanging genteel backchat with the plump manager, quizzing the customers. She knew everyone, knew all that was going on.

'Not seen your mother lately, love. Is she poorly?'

Jan looked and did not see her, picked up her bag and walked out.

Each night as she came home, Jan would fetch Kevin from next door, looking past the woman there with her broad, handsome face, hard hairdo and low neckline, into the cluttered kitchen with it's glaring TV, its haze of cigarette smoke, to call Kev from where he sat between her boys, pushing chocolate into his mouth.

'Mother poorly love?'

'Away.'

'Anytime you'd like me to pick up some shopping for you . . .'

'It's all right, thank you very much. We can manage. Kev are you coming?'

She did not know why she dragged her brother away. She did not even know why she rushed home, just to get his tea. But rush home she did, and dragged Kev away, for all his sullen looks and sometimes open grumbling. And she made him get undressed and into bed in good time, every night. Mum was 'away' for a while and everything was going on as though she were still here.

She would make cups of tea for Dad as he sat over his books. He did not drink them. But neither did he look at his books. He stared out of the window. And she returned to her room and opened her books and stared out at the darkening street below.

On Saturday as she stepped out of the front door, someone called her. It was old Mr Elsom from next door on the other side. A retired railwayman, he still wore a shabby, black waistcoat and collarless, flannel shirt. His crab-apple face was seamed and weathered, and when he stood close you could smell old man's sweat in his clothes.

He took her sleeve.

'Not seen your mother lately, love. I usually give her some potatoes at this

127

time of year. We've got plenty, Edie and I. Always help people, I say, never know when you may need it yourself.'

Help? What for? Jan thought she saw an inquisitive gleam in his eye.

'No thanks, we can manage.'

(The picture of his offended face went into the collection in Jan's head: Sharon, Miss Maudesley, other classmates, the supermarket lady, the woman next door – hurt expressions, raised eyebrows, half-open mouths. Sometimes, when she slept, these faces came and crowded round her, saying nothing, only staring, until she woke up in desperation.)

As the days passed she was aware that the burden of running the house had slipped on to her, that Dad was doing nothing but his course, coming home, eating a little, letting cups of tea go cold. He was doing nothing, allowing the days to pass, growing more silent, jumping when the phone rang. And it came into her mind that she should complain, speak to him, ask him what he was going to do. But she could not bring herself to throw off this heaviness, to lay herself open to things that might be worse.

One day, at break time, she leaned on the wall in the schoolyard. The faint warmth of the April sunshine comforted her somehow. Someone was talking to her. She stared. Tina Ellis was there bending close and speaking quietly:

'You all right, Jan?'

'Eh?' Tina Ellis and she had never spoken to one another. They'd shouted at each other, and once in the third year, they'd fought in the formroom, spilling stuff from the desks while the others cheered them on.

'Are you all right?'

'Course I am, what do you mean?'

Tina Ellis was silent, as though weighing up Jan's mood. Then she said: 'Our Mum cleared off – six months back.'

Jan pushed up from the wall.

'What are you talking about?' Her voice was hard. Tina's eyes widened.

'Nothing. Forget I said ought. Snob.'

She walked away, leaving Jan staring.

Robert Leeson

think

1 Pick out words and phrases which indicate how Jan feels about her mother leaving.
2 Write down your impressions of Kev and Jan's dad. Why do you think Jan is made the main character of the three?
3 The supermarket attendant, the neighbours and Tina Ellis all ask very similar questions of Jan. Why do you think they ask them?
4 What is it that Jan finds so difficult to accept in the attitudes of these people?

choose

a Write about another incident which might have taken place in Jan's life. Choose an area where people's attitudes make her feel like an outsider. Look carefully at the style in which the piece is written and try to imitate this type of language in your work.
b Imagine you are one of the people who tries to talk to Jan. How would you feel about her responses? Write a conversation that you might have with a friend later that day, as you describe the incident to them.
c Jan's mum is a character who is discussed at length, but never appears in the book. What sort of attitudes would she be likely to meet, having left her family and chosen to live away from them. Improvise and then write up a short play, which shows the sorts of attitudes others might have towards Jan's mum.

p152 d 'We can manage' is the reply Jan gives to all those who try to 'help' her. Do you think those people should have left Jan alone, or do we have a responsibility towards others? Write an argumentative piece giving your views on this subject.

 extra One on one

Thomas More was a statesman and a church minister in the reign of King Henry VIII. Henry wanted to divorce his first wife Catherine and marry Anne Boleyn. He wanted More's approval of the new marriage on oath. More did not approve, would not take the oath, and was eventually executed.

A Man For All Seasons by Robert Bolt, covers this period of Thomas More's life. Below is an extract from the play when More's family visit him in prison. Alice is More's wife and Margaret is his daughter. As you read, try to form a picture of the character of Thomas More.

Roper:	Yes. Meg's under oath to try to persuade you.
More:	*(coldly)* That was silly, Meg. How did you come to do that?
Margaret:	I wanted to!
More:	You want me to swear to the Act of Succession?
Margaret:	'God regards more the thoughts of the heart than the words of the mouth' or so you have always told me.
More:	Yes.
Margaret:	Then say the words of the oath and in your heart think otherwise.
More:	What is an oath but the words we say to God?
Margaret:	That's very neat.
More:	Do you mean it isn't true?
Margaret:	No, it's true.
More:	Then it's a poor argument to call it 'neat', Meg. When a man takes an oath, Meg, he's holding his own self in his own hands. Like water *(cups hands)* and if he opens his fingers *then* – he needn't hope to find himself again. Some men aren't capable of this, but I'd be loathe to think your father one of them.

*   *   *

Margaret:	*(emotional)* But in reason! Haven't you done as much as God can reasonably *want*?
More:	Well . . . finally . . . it isn't a matter of reason; finally it's a matter of love.
Alice:	*(hostile)* You're content then, to be shut up here with mice and rats when you might be at home with us!
More:	*(flinching)* Content? If they'd open a crack that wide *(between finger and thumb)* I'd be through it *(To Margaret)* Well has Eve run out of apples?
Margaret:	I've not told you what the house is like, without you.
More:	Don't Meg.
Margaret:	What we do in the evenings, now that you're not there.
More:	Meg have done!
Margaret:	We sit in the dark because we've no candles. And we've no talk because we're wondering what they're doing to you here.
More:	The King's more merciful than you. He doesn't use the rack.

*   *   *

More:	*(he is in fear of her)* I am faint when I think of the worst they may do to me. But worse than that would be to go, with you not understanding why I go.
Alice:	I don't!
More:	*(just hanging on to his self possession)* Alice, if you can tell me that you understand, I think I can make a good death, if I have to.
Alice:	Your death's no 'good' to me!
More:	Alice you must tell me that you understand!
Alice:	I don't *(She throws it straight at his head)* I don't believe this had to happen.
More:	*(his face is drawn)* If you say that Alice, I don't see how I am to face it.
Alice:	It's the truth!
More:	*(gasping)* You're an honest woman.
Alice:	Much good it may do me! I'l tell you what I'm afraid of; that when you've gone, I shall hate you for it.
More:	*(turns from her, his face is working)* Well, you mustn't, Alice, that's all. *(Swiftly she crosses the stage to him; he turns they clasp each other fiercely.)* You mustn't, you –
Alice:	*(covers his mouth with her hand)* S-s-sh . . . As for understanding, I understand you're the best man I ever met or am likely to; and if you go – well God knows why I suppose – though as God is my witness God's kept deadly quiet about it! And if anyone wants my opinion of the King and his Council they've only to ask for it!
More:	Why, it's a lion I married! A lion! A lion! *(He breaks away from her his face shining.)*

Robert Bolt

The following passage gives Robert Bolt's explanatory notes on *A Man For All Seasons* with particular reference to the meaning of the oath.

More was a very orthodox Catholic and for him an oath was something perfectly specific; it was an invitation to God, an invitation God would not refuse, to act as a witness, and to judge; the consequence of perjury was damnation, for More another perfectly specific concept. So for More the issue was simple (though remembering the outcome it can hardly have been easy). But I am not a Catholic nor even in a meaningful sense of the word a Christian. So by what right do I appropriate a Christian Saint to my purposes? Or to put it another way, why do I take as my hero a man who brings about his own death because he can't put his hand on an old black book and tell an ordinary lie?

For this reason: A man takes an oath only when he wants to commit himself quite exceptionally to the statement, when he wants to make an identity between the truth of it and his own virtue; he offers himself as a guarantee. And it works. There is a special kind of shrug for a perjurer; we feel that the man has no self to commit, no guarantee to offer.

Most men feel when they make an oath (the marriage vow for example) that they have invested something. And from this it's possible to guess what an oath must be to a man for whom it is not merely a time-honoured and understood ritual but also a definite contract.

think **1** Write down, in your own words, the meaning of the following phrases in the context of the passage:
- 'he's holding his own self in his hands. Like water and if he opens his fingers then he needn't hope to find himself again.'
- 'Well has Eve run out of apples?'
- 'The king's more merciful than you. He doesn't use the rack.'

2 What impressions do you get of Margaret and Alice? What else do you find out about More by looking at their speech and actions.

3 What are your overall impressions of More? Note down five things which you feel sum up his character.

4 Explain briefly, in your own words, what you think taking the oath meant to Thomas More. Use both passages as reference.

choose **a** Carry out a piece of role play in the form of an interview with Thomas More. He might talk about Henry VIII, or, having been transported to the present day, about some more modern issues.

p174 **b** Imagine that More has to write a letter to Alice and Margaret, after his meeting, telling them why he is refusing to take the oath. Use all the information you can glean from the two passages to write that letter.

p156 **c** Alice is at home later in the evening and decides to demand some answers from God. Write down the prayer you think she might speak.

d Write a report on More's character as you see it. Discuss and write about his relationship with Alice and Margaret. Do you see him as admirable or foolish?

1 An overview of your file

What should be in your file?

Your GCSE file should show the examiner the *flexibility* of your writing and the *breadth* of your abilities. You need to write in each of the following *modes*:

Argumentative/Persuasive

Descriptive

Late Home

The road narrowed and curved. On either side were high, unkempt hawthorn hedges and behind them the remains of old chalk quarries: large white sores that wouldn't heal. Headlights swept towards her. She kept her hands steady and her eyes rigidly on the air just to the left of the lights. At such times she always felt that she had become invisible to the other driver, who would only realise her existence after the impact. The lorry swept past: a gust of hot air and diesel fumes and total unconcern.

Trevor Millum

The French Lieutenant's Woman

She turned and sat quickly and gracefully sideways on a hammock several feet in front of the tree, so that she turned and faced the sea: and so, as Charles found when he took the better seat, that her face was half hidden from him — and yet again, by some ingenious coquetry, so that he must take note of her hair. She sat very upright, yet with head bowed, occupied in an implausible adjustment of her bonnet. Charles watched her, with a smile in his mind if not on his lips. He would see she was at a loss how to begin: and yet the situation was too *al fresco*, too informally youthful, as if they were a boy and sister, for the shy formality she betrayed.

John Fowles

Letter Writing

Sir, — In considering and rejecting the arguments against tactical voting by socialists in order to prevent the return of a government headed by Mrs Thatcher Prof Eric Hobsbawm (Agenda, April 24) omits consideration of what is surely the most powerful argument : that in a democracy a person ought to vote in accordance with his or her settled political convictions, to vote *for* a party, not against one.

It is not at all obvious that the return of Mrs Thatcher after a general election would be a *betrayal* of democracy, as Prof Hobsbawm alleges, but it is arguable that tactical voting is. For if it succeeds, or even if it is thought to have succeeded, whichever political grouping forms the next government does so with feigned support ; but it is faced by an Opposition which has genuine support. This consequence will not have been lost on Neil Kinnock, I imagine.

The Guardian

MARKS & CO., Booksellers
84, Charing Cross Road
London, W.C.2

Miss Helene Hanff
14 East 95th Street
New York 28, New York
U.S.A.

1ST NOVEMBER, 1950

Dear Miss Hanff,

I am sorry for the delay in answering your letter but I have been away out of town for a week or so and am now busy trying to catch up on my correspondence.

First of all, please don't worry about us using old books such as Clarendon's Rebellion for wrapping. In this particular case they were just two odd volumes with the covers detached and nobody in their right senses would have given us a shilling for them.

The Quiller-Couch anthology, *The Pilgrim's Way*, has been sent to you by Book Post. The balance due was $1.85 so your $2 more than covered it. We haven't a copy of Pepys' *Diary* in stock at the moment but shall look out for one for you.

With best wishes,
Yours faithfully,

F. Doel
For MARKS & CO.

Narrative

The Loneliness of a Long-Distance Runner

As soon as I got to Borstal they made me a long-distance cross-country runner. I suppose they thought I was just the build for it because I was long and skinny for my age (and still am) and in any case I didn't mind it much, to tell you the truth, because running had always been made much of in our family, especially running away from the police. I've always been a good runner, quick and with a big stride as well, the only trouble being that no matter how fast I run, and I did a very fair lick even though I do say so myself, it didn't stop me getting caught by the cops after that bakery job.

Alan Silitoe

The L-Shaped Room

There wasn't much to be said for the place, really, but it had a roof over it an a door which locked from the inside, which was all I cared about just then. I didn't even bother to take in the detail they were pretty sordid, but I didn't notice them so they didn't depress me; perhaps because I was already at rock-bottom. I just threw my one suitcase on to the bed, took my few belongings out o it and shut them all into one drawer of the three-legged chest of drawers. Then there didn't seem to be anything else I ought to do so I sat in the arm-chair and stared out of the window.

Lynne Reed Bank

Instructive and Report Writing

<u>Report on Survey.</u>

We conducted a survey in a mixed class of 15 year olds, to find out how people viewed their relationship with their brothers and sisters.

Review

Street Scene

THE intelligent musical or serious operetta has been around a long time — as Kurt Weill, with his updated Beggars' Opera, knew very well. Nobody now criticises The Magic Flute for its mixture of styles and forms : it's all Mozart to us. I believe it's time we recognised Street Scene as all Weill and not a product of imagined artistic compromise.

Why should theatre audiences, fed recently on a diet of musicals devoid of music, not be allowed a work of this quality and passionate intensity ? There was no dress rehearsal for Sunday's Aids gala, but Street Scene was triumphantly vindicated. It works. You emerge singing the tunes, with no feeling they are a cynical plea for popularity and success, rather than strictly functional.

A huge cast-list comes to memorable life, each character confidently outlined in musical terms. Weill uses all the tricks of the Broadway musical to achieve his accessible social realism, but he breaks all the rules too.

As treated by Weill, Elmer Rice's slice of life drama is a cantata about the dreams and ambitions of ordinary people longing for a better future. The stresses of poverty are plain, though the better-off have problems too.

When Anna Maurant is shot by her insensitive husband, caught in flagrante with her lover, he is destroying a universal dream of escape — not just avenging a conventional affront (sex is the opium of the masses, even such a " pure " form as suggested here). Weill gives Anna wonderful material to suggest indelibly her role as enslaved visionary at the slum's heart. And Hilary Western relished the challenge of " Somehow I never could believe."

Inevitably a rushed job like this gala could not meet all the challenges — such as where the weight of climax comes in the longest numbers. But John Owen Edwards's preparation and conducting achieved a miraculously high level.

The Guardian

Watching brief

HIS VOICE HIS WRITTEN WORD (BBC-2, 9 55). Young Irish writer Christopher Nolan had his first book out at 15 and this week, aged 21, his autobiography — Under The Eye Of The Clock — is published. The remarkable thing is that he suffered brain damage at birth and can neither walk nor speak. The devastating lack of a link between his intellect and its normal means of expression has been overcome by laborious use of a typewriter with a stick attached to his forehead. Covering his work presented a challenge to producer Jenny Cowan but Christy had clear ideas about how it should be presented. His new book, focus of tonight's programme, reflects his difficult world and reveals a strangely poised detachment from himself.

135

2

Ways of writing

Drafting

A good piece of work is very rarely written in one draft. This isn't just true for school writing, but also in the 'real' world of professional writers. Below is an extract from an article by Adèle Geras which shows the type of redrafting carried out by professional writers:

Whether teenagers need special 'teenage' fiction written for them is one of the questions that greatly exercise publishers and writers. It's a fact that many of you read adult books of all kinds and therefore shouldn't feel yourselves confined to 'Upstarts' but should also seek out the many books you would enjoy among the dark-green Viragos, or anywhere else. You can't divide good fiction into rigid age-bands. It ought to be capable of crossing lots of barriers, not least that of age. However, on to Virago's non-fiction.

Many people can dash off a reasonable piece at one go, but the type of file work demanded for GCSE needs your time and patience in redrafting.

Here is a useful drafting procedure:

Essay title: **Describe what you did yesterday**

Notes:
A basic summary of what should be included, perhaps a blitz of ideas to get you thinking.

Got up early / did Physics homework before school / missed bus / late to school / normal day – French, History, English, Physics, Maths / had to stay in detention for being late / watched T.V.

1st draft:
Your first attempt to make the notes into real sentences.

Yesterday I got up early. I did my Physics homework and then went to school. I missed the bus and arrived at school late. The lessons yesterday were French, History, English and Physics and Maths. After school I had to stop behind for a detention for being late. When I got home I watched T.V.

Get someone else's honest opinion. This could be a classmate, parent, brother, teacher.

It isn't very personal yet, I don't really get the impression that you're involved.
Why not tell me about your feelings through the day?
It's rather short and I don't feel as if you're describing a real person, it could be a robot's day.

137

2nd draft:
Your first attempts to shape the writing in order to meet the criticisms made.

Yesterday I got up early. I had to; I'd watched the T.V. all night on Monday and my Physics homework still had to be done. I rushed it off and ran for the bus, but missed it. Mr Baxter saw me coming in late and demanded a detention, just my luck! Normal boring Tuesday today: French, History, English, Physics and Maths. I tried to skip home but Baxter was waiting outside the Maths class ready to pounce. I was a bit annoyed to miss Grange Hill, but I watched T.V. for the rest of the evening anyway.

Get someone else's honest opinion. Ask them for a full critical report.

I don't think the bit about T.V. is important. I'd rather hear more about the lessons.
You are beginning to make this feel real with your feelings towards Mr Baxter — why not tell me more about him.

3rd draft:
This may take the form of writing the piece out again, but is more likely to involve, a great deal of crossing out and changing of your 2nd Draft.

Yesterday I got up early. I had to; I'd watched the T.V. all night on Monday and my Physics homework still had to be done. I rushed it off and ran for the bus, but missed it. Mr Baxter saw me coming in late and

↪ with old 'fruit bat', we call her that because she squeaks and can't see straight; demanded a detention, just my luck! Normal boring Tuesday today: French*, History**, English***, Physics**** and Maths. I tried to skip home but Baxter was waiting outside the Maths Class ready to pounce. ~~I was a bit annoyed to~~ we call him the terrible tiger ~~miss Grange Hill, but I watched T.V. for the~~ because he waits in corridors looking for first years ~~rest of the evening anyway.~~ like raw meat.

↪ on the Viking invasion, I can't say I was enthralled, as we did it in the first year!
*** and another session of Dickens, I suppose it's getting a bit better.
**** Everyone had done the homework so it's a good thing I did.

Yesterday I got up early. I had to, I'd watched the T.V. all night on Monday and my Physics homework still had to be done. I rushed it off and ran for the bus, but missed it. Mr Baxter saw me coming in late and demanded a detention, just my luck!

Assessment: Your teacher doesn't always need to be involved in the marking of this work until it has reached its final draft. Learning to assess and improve your own work is important so that you become more independent in your writing.

Punctuation

The correct use of punctuation enables us to read writing more easily. The following passages are intended to show the correct use of punctuation. Read them through carefully, and check them off against the skills reminders which are noted alongside.

Capital letters
1 For a person's name.
2 For the beginning of a sentence.
3 For a place name.
4 For a person's title.
5 For book titles.
6 For months of the year.
7 For abbreviations.
8 For the makes and names of ships, boats and for brand names.
9. For street names.

¹John walked down the road. ²He didn't feel any different, but things certainly had changed. It was certainly true that ³Paris was unlike any other city, and ⁴Mr Howes had been right about the money too. He would have to read the book again "⁵A Personal Guidebook to Paris" wasn't that the name? It was ⁶April, early spring, the same season as back in the ⁷U.S.A., and yet how different it felt here, with the ⁸Jaguars sweeping down the ⁹Champs Elysees!

Full stop
1 For abbreviations (no need for a full stop if the word abbreviated ends in the last letter of the word. i.e. mister – Mr doctor – Dr).
2 At the end of a sentence.

The meeting was held on Monday Sept. 14th, as had been expected.

Question mark and exclamation mark
1 A question mark is used at the end of a question in direct speech. It is not usually used in reported speech.
2 An exclamation mark is used to show shock, amusement, or indicate shouting.

'Where are you going?' Jan asked. She said she was going to the shops and asked if it was any of her business. 'Well!' Jan spluttered, unable to say any more.

Comma

Used to mark off words of a minor clause, in a similar way to a bracket.

Used to prevent confusion in the sentence: he woke up his eyes . . .

Between the words in a list.

To show a break in direct speech.

Gail[1], the doctor on the ward[2], could only show surprise. He had said that when he woke up[2], his eyes were streaming. There was John[3], Katie, Joe, and Steve, all of whom he might have suspected, but David was so young. 'Did he realise what he was doing?' 'I suppose[4],' he said 'he thought it was a joke'.

Colon/semi-colon

Colon used to introduce a list.

Colon used to introduce a long piece of direct speech.

Semi-colon used between two parts of a sentence which are linked closely, but which could stand as separate sentences.

A semi-colon can be used to separate items on a list, when the items are longer than one word.

He packed the sandwich box carefully[1]: a ham sandwich, an egg sandwich, yesterday's apple and a fresh orange. He stopped and said[2]: 'You know, I don't like to complain, but there are three people in this house, and yet I always make the sandwiches. Can't someone else try?' There was no reply[3]; everyone had left already.

'A quiet life is all I'm after[1]: someone to organize my business[4]; a chance to go out and walk[4]; someone else to make the sandwiches!'

Apostrophe
1 Used to show that a letter is missing.
It is – it's
I have – I've
2 To show that something belongs to someone.
(The possessions belonging to his mother – his mother's possessions. Here used in the singular (one mother). If plural, the apostrophe follows the 's'. The boys' voices (several boys). 'Its' is an exception. Its neck – there is no possessive appostrophe used here.

'It's OK I've found it!' He had been shouting from the attic for so long, that his brother took no notice of this latest piece of news. 'These were my mother's most treasured possessions.' He was at the top of the stairs now, leaning over the bannisters. 'Yes, and those are my mother's eyes,' he thought, looking up into his brother's excited face.

Speech marks
1 Speech marks surround the words spoken directly by the person. All punctuation relating to the words spoken, goes inside the speech marks. ('What do you want?')
2 A new line is started for each new speaker, but there is no need to start a new line if the same speaker, speaks again.
3 A comma, or some other form of punctuation should come before each piece of speech, unless the words spoken start a new line.

"What do you want?" he said.
"There's no need to snap, I...'
' You nothing, you're not welcome here and you should know it by now,' he frowned. well, what is it?'

Paragraphing

Paragraphs break up a piece of writing into smaller units. This may be to speed up or slow the pace of a piece of writing; to place stress on a particular word, phrase, or sentence; to separate different ideas in a passage, or to tell a story in easily understandable sections. Therefore, where you put paragraphs is a very personal decision. There are no *rules* for correct paragraphing, but there are *conventions*.

Below are three different types of writing, each using a different formula for paragraphing.

Newspaper Article

Newspaper articles usually have a punchy, fast-paced style because the author needs to keep her/his story moving. This is achieved by short paragraphs.

Paragraph 1 – a very short paragraph causes impact, and pulls the reader's attention immediately into the article.

Paragraph 3 – gives more background to the story. It explains further paragraphs 1 and 2, but remains short to give a fast pace to the article.

Paragraph 4 – places the issue in the present time, rather than the past, as it has been up to now.

Paragraphs 5 and 6 – continue to tell the story, dividing it into easily digestible chunks.

TOP local celebrities this week joined together with a band of angry residents who have mounted a campaign to stop the axe from falling on the popular Chalk Farm library.

Actress Gayle Hunnicutt, top journalist Simon Jenkins and well known novelist Mervyn Jones are among the signatories to a letter of protest sent to the New Journal this week which is part of a bid to prevent Camden Council from going ahead with the closure (see page 4).

They have also signed a petition which will be presented to the council's ruling Labour group. It will also be signed by hundreds of children from local schools who use the library.

A proposed package of library cuts — which included the closure of St Pancras, Chalk Farm, High Holborn, Kilburn and Belsize libraries — was due to have been decided on at a Labour Group meeting earlier this week, but it was postponed until Monday.

Mervyn Jones told the New Journal: "I was very shocked to hear about the closure and I have no wish to walk to Swiss Cottage in future. It will be particularly difficult for elderly people wanting to use the library.

"As a novelist I hope people will take the trouble to read books and at current prices not many people can afford to. That is why libraries have such an important role to play."

Avis Hutt, one of the protest letter's signatories and chairwoman of the Primrose Hill Neighbours Help group, said: "It's appalling that the council should even consider closing libraries.

"Our library is an extremely important community facility."

Another signatory Mollie Dixon, a retired teacher, said: "It's absolutely crucial that people be given access to books. They play such an important role in the development of thinking people."

A statement by the Chalk Farm Labour Party urges the council to cut down library hours across the borough rather than close down some libraries entirely.

It says: "The closure of Chalk Farm library would mean particular difficulties for local residents: some hundreds of senior citizens on the Oldfield estate who would be faced with a long walk or problems of public transport to neighbouring libraries; the toddler group and pre-school group based at the library, and the 450 children attending Primrose Hill Primary school."

The Camden New Journal

143

Fiction

Styles of fiction writing vary, but generally speaking, novels don't need so fast a pace as newspaper articles. Paragraphs can afford to be longer, to give more detail, and to allow the reader to enter more deeply into the writing.

In the Shadow of the Wind

Paragraph 1 – this is a long paragraph. The style of the book is that of 'stream of consciousness' (the continuous thoughts of the character who is narrating the story). The narrator almost drifts off into describing the sights and sounds nearby.

In autumn when the snow geese leave this corner of the world by the thousands for more clement skies, I hear their honking up above the house, high up in the gloom. The perfect shadow of their formations passes through the shingled roof as if it were transparent and alights on my quilt, fleeting black geometry. I could touch them with my hand. Lying on my bed, my sisters asleep in the enclosed room, my ears alert, I sense a sort of muffled barking far away. If I get up, barefoot, and lift the cretonne curtain, crane my neck and raise my head, I see the sky covered with birds in full flight, like regiments deployed by night. The evenly shaped v moves at the speed of the wind.

Paragraph 2 – brings the reader back into the immediate situation in the bedroom, and to the dreams of the narrator.

Back in the warmth of my bed, the sheets pulled up to my chin, eyes shut, I wonder which of these wild birds, under cover of what dense darkness, will alight on my roof one evening, in the course of its journey. A swan. I'm sure it will be a swan. His plumage will open, I'll see his naked heart, beating only for me. Then all at once he'll shed his white feathers, and they'll rise in a snowy mound at his feet. His form, that of a man set free from a spell that was crushing him. His face the pure face of a crowned king. No other girl in the world will be loved, will love, more than I, Nora Atkins. I dream. I sleep. Love. Unless he were to come by sea, from one of those passing foreign ships, decked out in every colour, their poignant foghorns under clumps of cotton wool. He lands. He sets foot on the shore, takes me in his arms, carries me away, and nails me to the front of his pirate's ship. A figurehead for eternity, my small breasts frosted with salt, the waves slapping my face, and I can't wipe them away. Most likely he'll come along the yellow sandy road, in a cloud of dust. All the nickel on his car glittering in the sun. A Chevrolet or a Buick. What's important is that it's new and glistening, with soft cushions and a whining horn. Americans sometimes come like that, in summer, looking at us like strange animals while the beauty of our landscape seals their lips and freezes their souls.

Anne Herber

Letters

The conventions for paragraphing in letters are tighter, particularly in a formal letter. A new paragraph is needed for each new point made, as well as a clear introductory and summarizing paragraph.

Paragraph 1 – is an introductory paragraph which refers to the previous letter as a 'politeness' convention.

Paragraph 2 – is the main part of the letter, explaining what the writer has done in response to the previous letter.

Paragraph 3 – is a summary of what he intends to do next, thus 'signing off' until the next letter.

MARKS & CO., Booksellers
84, Charing Cross Road
London, W.C.2

1ST NOVEMBER, 1950

Miss Helene Hanff
14 East 95th Street
New York 28, New York
U.S.A.

Dear Miss Hanff,

I am sorry for the delay in answering your letter but I have been away out of town for a week or so and am now busy trying to catch up on my correspondence.

First of all, please don't worry about us using old books such as Clarendon's Rebellion for wrapping. In this particular case they were just two odd volumes with the covers detached and nobody in their right senses would have given us a shilling for them.

The Quiller-Couch anthology, *The Pilgrim's Way*, has been sent to you by Book Post. The balance due was $1.85 so your $2 more than covered it. We haven't a copy of Pepys' *Diary* in stock at the moment but shall look out for one for you.

With best wishes,
Yours faithfully,

F. Doel
For MARKS & CO.

Note-taking

During the course you will need to take notes to:

- keep an account of a discussion
- glean necessary information from a book
- organize your ideas for a piece of oral work
- organize your ideas for a piece of written work

You need to develop your own most effective method for keeping notes. The following are a selection of methods, with ideas for making them work. You will need to try out a few ideas before deciding which to use in any given situation.

The Spider Graph

This is useful for initial planning. It depends upon there being links between subjects, but it is useable in most types of note-taking. It can get very messy on the page, but it does allow you to add to it later.

Task: *Research the historical background to Shakespeare's writing.*

Star Blitz

This is useful for the earliest stage of discussion work. The Star Blitz allows you to get your initial ideas flowing. It doesn't show connections between ideas, and it depends upon you remembering chosen key words, used to represent ideas.

Task: *What is meant by human rights?*

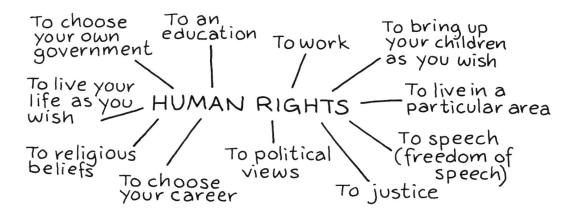

Comparative Columns

This is most useful for comparative or argumentative discussion or essay work. It leads very naturally into longer written work, although not all arguments divide neatly into two.

Task: *Should the police be armed?*

YES	NO
– Criminals are armed.	– Can be fired incorrectly by accident.
– Police are highly trained.	– Encourages more violence from police and public.
– In the USA they are already, and in some other countries.	– Makes the country feel oppressed.
– Without them police are "sitting ducks".	– Condones violence in society.
– Trained to wound not kill.	– Endangers the public – crossfire.

Noting the Main Points

This is a most useful way of recording just the bare bones of a passage or discussion. It leads naturally into fuller writing but means that a great deal of time must be spent in the selection of the points to note.

Task: *Record how you bake a cake.*

1. Measure 100g flour, 100g sugar, 100g butter
2. Beat 4 eggs.
3. Cream butter and sugar until white.
4. Beat in flour and eggs gradually.
5. Place in greased tin.
6. Place in 180°c oven for 30 minutes.

Recording Longhand as Shorthand

This involves writing words in a shorter form. It is useful if you want to record someone's exact words or to make longer, more detailed notes. One way of taking notes in shorthand is to miss out any vowels, to substitute numbers for words i.e. to = 2, for = 4, and to abbreviate names. You do have to practise to do it well, and make sure that you don't forget your own shorthand!

Task: *What were the opinions of miners on the 1984 strike?*

Mr Smith: 'My wf I can't surv. 4 much longr, we nd to shw tht we can't take it sit'g dwn.'

Mrs Smith: 'We usd 2b a close fmly, but we hv bn drvn 2 our kns.'

Flow Chart

This is particularly useful for planning a talk, where different people are involved, or for showing a sequence of ideas. It is an immediate visual reminder, but takes some time to present clearly.

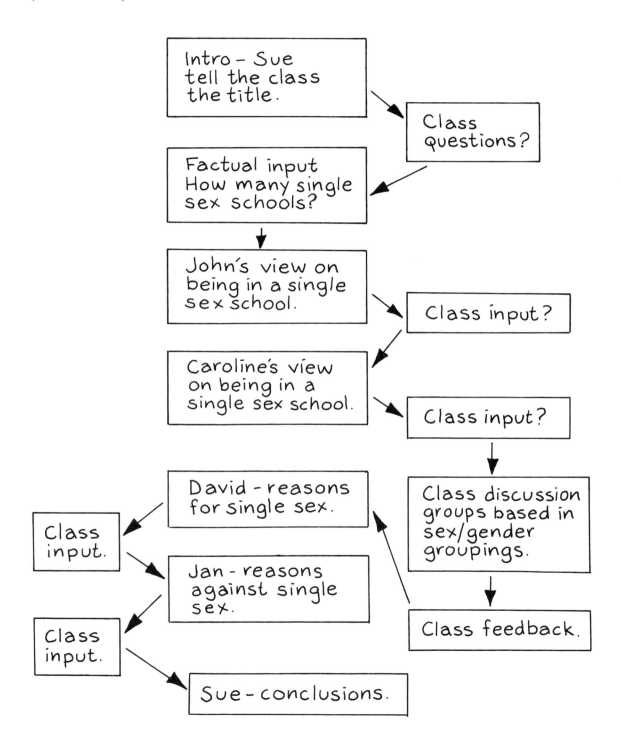

Vocabulary Extension

Reading

The answer to the question, 'How do I increase my vocabulary?' is to read widely from a wide variety of sources. You will soon find that the words you've seen written are subtly sneaking their way into your vocabulary.

Looking at a Thesaurus

Another, quicker approach is to use a Thesaurus. The easiest way to use a Thesaurus is to find one word for what you mean (eg honest) and then look it up in the back section.

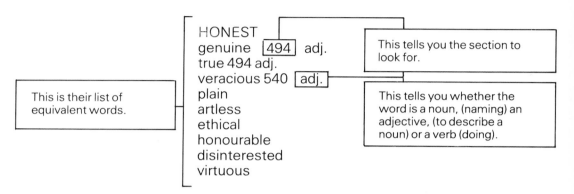

HONEST
genuine 494 adj.
true 494 adj.
veracious 540 adj.
plain
artless
ethical
honourable
disinterested
virtuous

This tells you the section to look for.

This is their list of equivalent words.

This tells you whether the word is a noun, (naming) an adjective, (to describe a noun) or a verb (doing).

Then look up the word which most nearly matches your meaning, by turning to the section number referred to. Here you will find several alternative words and phrases with the same, or a similar meaning.

VERACIOUS
truthful . . . trustworthy . . . straightforward . . . scrupulous . . .

Armed with this selection of alternatives to your one original word, you can angle your piece of writing to the *style* you feel is appropriate. Style, after all, is simply an expression of choice, choosing one word or phrase, instead of another.

An Honest Man

Mr Parker was an honest man. Indeed his veracity knew no bounds. Faced with the eternal question, 'Should I go to the ticket office and buy a rail ticket for a journey I've made without one?' his answer was reliably unembroidered. 'Of course, it would be just untruthful to do otherwise!' He is indeed a 'man of honour'.

Here, instead of repeating the word honesty or honest, other words, with similar meaning have been used:

- veracity
- reliably unembroidered
- truthful
- man of honour

and the passage avoids being repetitive and dull.

Learning New Words

Another useful approach is to set yourself targets of words to learn. You could try keeping a note of any new words you come across in newspapers, magazines and books, or from conversations and television.

To avoid mis-spelling

The following are believed to be the most commonly mis-spelt words in English. You could try to learn ten a week.

absence	college	familiar	Mediterranean	psychology
accidentally	coming	February	miniature	quiet
accommodate	committee	financial	minutes	really
achieved	comparative	forty	mischievous	received
acknowledge	competent	friend	murmur	recommended
acquainted	completely	fulfilled		referred
addresses	conscientious		necessary	relieved
aerial	conscious	gauge	negotiate	repetition
aggravate	consistent	genius	niece	restaurant
agreeable	convenience	government	noticeable	rhythm-ic
all right	courteous	grammar	occasional	
amateur	courtesy	grievance	occasionally	scarcely
among	criticism	guard	occurred	secretaries
analysis		guardian	occurrence	seize
Antarctic	deceive	handkerchief	omission	sentence
anxiety	decision	height	omitted	separate
apparent	definite	heroes	opinion	severely
appearance	desirable	honorary	originally	shining
appropriate	desperate	humorous		similar
Arctic	disappeared	hungry	parallel	sincerely
argument	disappointed	hurriedly	parliament	statutory
arrangements	disastrous	hypocrisy	pastime	successfully
ascend	discipline	imagination	permanent	supersede
athletic	dissatisfied	immediately	permissible	suppression
automation		immigrate	perseverance	surprising
awful	efficiency	incidentally	personnel	synonymous
	eighth	independent	physical	
bachelor	eliminated	indispensable	planning	tendency
beginning	embarrassed	influential	pleasant	tragedy
believed	emphasize(s)	intelligence	possession	transferred
beneficial	enthusiasm	irresistible	preceding	twelfth
benefited	equipped	knowledge	preference	unconscious
breathe	especially		prejudice	undoubtedly
budgeted	essential	liaison	preliminary	unnecessary
business	exaggerated	literature	prestige	until
ceiling	excellent	livelihood	privilege	usually
certain	exercise	lose	procedure	
choice	exhausted	losing	proceeds	valuable
clothes	existence	lying	profession	view
colleagues	expenses	maintenance	professor	Wednesday
	experience	marriage	pronunciation	woollen
	extremely	medicine	proprietary	

To avoid confusion

Here are a series of words which sound the same, but which have a different meaning. They are known as 'homophones'. Check you know their meaning by making up a sentence using each one.

court caught	pain pane	prey pray	some sum	through threw
die dye	pair pare pear	prise prize	sort sought	troop troupe
flour flower	pale pail	rain reign rein	sow sew	vale veil
its it's	pier peer	rapt wrapped	stationary stationery	waive wave
led lead	plaice place	root route	steal steel	wear where
	plane plain	shear sheer	stile style	weather whether
or ore oar	plum plumb	sight site	sty stye	week weak
	pore poor pour	soar sore	their there they're	

151

3

Modes of writing

Argumentative and Persuasive Writing

Part of a writer's skill is the ability to change their reader's viewpoint by showing a clear argument and through persuasion. There are several different types of persuasive writing:

The Didactic Approach   The Gentle Balancing Trick   The Fact Giver

Before you begin planning you need to know how you intend to angle your argument. For each of the approaches above, you need to have certain information and to have decided on the most appropriate organization.

Choices
What is *your* viewpoint?

Even if you intend to present a balanced essay, you need to decide what *your* views on the subject are. Your views may creep into essays unconsciously.

Should the police be armed?

Where will you be in the essay?

Inside	**Outside**
Arguing a personal view in a powerful voice.	Not taking a viewpoint, but presenting different views on the subject.
Subjective	Objective
Biased	Unbiased
Emotive language using many persuasive words.	Detached, non-emotive language, using few persuasive words.
Less of others' views.	Several views expressed.

What is the factual information you could use?

- the number of police killed at work;
- incidents of accidents when police are armed;
- public opinion polls on the issue;
- newspaper articles/TV documentaries which you can quote or refer to.

Organization

It is useful to write down all the possible points for and against an argument:
Should the police be armed?

For	Against
Criminals are often armed.	Are police officers adequately trained?
Police officers are placed in dangerous situations.	Split-second decisions have to be made, and this places undue stress on officers.
Police officers are 'sitting ducks' to armed criminals.	Several accidents have taken place where innocent people have been wounded or killed.
Statistical evidence.	Statistical evidence.

Decisions of ordering

There are several ways to order an argument in order to make it more balanced, or persuasive. Here are three ideas:

You can select one 'for' and then one 'against' the argument throughout the essay.

You can argue one side of the argument and then the other.

You can undermine one point by following it by another stronger point, in order to stress one argument more than the other.

Beginnings and endings

This is the point in the essay when you can be the most *personal*. You need to summarize the issues *clearly*, whether you decide to aim for subjectivity or objectivity. You might decide to save an argument, for or against, to the end in order to give a strong punchline.

Tasks

Select one of the following titles to plan an argumentative essay, as suggested in this section. Work with a partner and decide on a strong basis for the argument you choose. Then, write up the essay:

- Everyone should be paid the same.
- Politics should be kept out of schools.
- There should be no single sex schools.
- We should increase this country's taxes in order to fund developing countries.
- Children's rights are more important than parent's rights.
- There should be a death penalty for murder.
- Schools should be run by students.

Descriptive Writing

Most types of writing demand a certain amount of description, which gives an idea of the look or feel of a place or person.

Below are three different types of description. One appeals to sight, one to the sense of smell, and the other to an emotional level.

Rebecca

Last night I dreamt I went to Manderley again. It seemed to me I stood by the iron gate leading to the drive, and for a while I could not enter for the way was barred to me. There was a padlock and a chain upon the gate. I called in my dream to the lodge-keeper, and had no answer, and peering closer through the rusted spokes of the gate I saw that the lodge was uninhabited.

No smoke came from the chimney, and the little lattice windows gaped forlorn. Then, like all dreamers, I was possessed of a sudden with supernatural powers and passed like a spirit through the barrier before me. The drive wound away in front of me, twisting and turning as it had always done, but as I advanced I was aware that a change had come upon it; it was narrow and unkept, not the drive that we had known.

Daphne du Maurier

The Amazing Mr Blunden

Clumps of herbs had spread from the garden into the ruins: thyme and marjoram which gave off a sweet, wet scent underfoot. There were wallflowers too, high up on the stonework, and she added to her basket the few that were within reach.

Beyond the ruins, a gravel path wound its way into the shrubbery and she went on in search of the rhododendron. She smelt it before she saw it, a thick, honey scent filling the air, and then round a corner she found the big pale-pink blossoms against dark leaves.

She picked half-a-dozen and then stood idly, breathing in the rich perfume. The air was noisy with birds and she could see through a gap in the bushes the bright green of the lawns with the crowding trees beyond. The heat of the spring sunshine was drying up the heavy rainfall which rose in patches of mist above the grass.

Lucy began to feel strangely drowsy as though the scent of the rhododendron were a sweet, heavy drug. Her mind seemed to be growing still and empty almost as if it had stuck in a groove from which she was unable to move it.

Antonia Barber

Bleak House

Fog everywhere. Fog up the river, where it flows among green aits and meadows; fog down the river, where it rolls defiled among the tiers of shipping, and the waterside pollutions of a great (and dirty) city. Fog on the Essex marshes, fog on the Kentish heights. Fog creeping into the cabooses of collier-brigs; fog lying out on the yards, and hovering in the rigging of great ships; fog drooping on the gunwales of barges and small boats. Fog in the eyes and throats of ancient Greenwich pensioners, wheezing by the firesides of their wards; fog in the stem and bowl of the afternoon pipe of the wrathful skipper, down in his close cabin; fog cruelly pinching the toes and fingers of his shivering little 'prentice boy on deck. Chance people on the bridges peeping over the parapets into a nether sky of fog, with fog all round them, as if they were up in a balloon, and hanging in the misty clouds.

And hard by Temple Bar, in Lincoln's Inn Hall, at the very heart of the fog, sits the Lord High Chancellor in his High Court of Chancery.

Charles Dickens

When writing a description there are several techniques which can be employed:
- observing closely;
- 'seeing' through the five senses: sound, smell, touch, taste, sight;
- focusing on the specifics of a scene;
- choosing specific (perhaps emotive) vocabulary.

In poetry a writer's choices are more obviously visible. Some writers create their effect by the use of multiple adjectives and adverbs:

Pied Beauty

Glory be to God for dappled things –
For skies of couple-colour as a brinded cow;
For rose-moles all in stipple upon trout that swim;
Fresh-firecoal chestnut-falls; finches' wings:
Landscape plotted and pieced – fold, fallow, and plough;
And all trades, their gear and tackle and trim.

All things counter, original, spare, strange;
Whatever is fickle, freckled (who knows how?)
With swift, slow; sweet, sour; adazzle, dim;
He fathers-forth whose beauty is past change:
Praise him.

Gerard Manly Hopkins

Others create their effects by a small number of adjectives and a high density of nouns:

Nights in the Iron Hotel

Our beds are at a hospital distance.
I push them together. Straw matting
on the walls produces a Palm Beach effect:
long drinks made with rum in tropical bars.
The position of mirror and wardrobe
recalls a room I once lived in happily.
Our feelings are shorter and faster now.
You confess a new infidelity. This time,
a trombone player. His tender mercies . . .
All night, we talk about separating.
The radio wakes us with its muzak.
In a sinister way, you call it lulling.
We are fascinated by our own anaesthesia,
our inability to function. Sex is a luxury,
an export of healthy physical economies.
The TV stays switched on all the time.
Dizzying social realism for the drunks.
A gymnast swings like a hooked fish.

Prague
Michael Hofmann

Descriptions are useful to try to take readers further into a story, so that they feel as if they are actually seeing and experiencing the scene.

Letter Writing

The Skills Section on paragraphing, on page 145, will give you some ideas about the internal structure of a formal letter.

When writing a letter you need first to decide the level of formality, and judge the correct tone for the letter.

Type of letter	Tone	e.g.
An application for a job.	polite, intelligent, clear	Dear Sir/Madam, I wish to apply for the post of assistant technician, as advertised in the B.B.C. . .
A letter of complaint to the local council.	forceful, persuasive	Dear Sir/Madam, I should like to express displeasure at the dismissal of my colleague of twenty years.
A letter explaining an absence from school.	clear, accurate, concise	Dear Mr Baxter, John was absent from school yesterday, as he has a bit of a cold. I'd be grateful if he could be . . .
A memorandum to a colleague.	brief and to the point	John, Have you ordered the new stock of A4 paper? It's vital that you do so now, if you have not already.
A postcard to a friend.	fairly informal, descriptive	Dear Ian, I am having a great time here in Cornwall. The weather is amazing and we have been surfing . . .
A letter to a close friend.	intimate, humorous(?), personal	Dear Sue, I'm sorry about the outburst the other night. Let me explain why I was in such a foul temper . . .
A note left at home to explain why you have gone out.	brief, perhaps almost 'coded' in family jargon	Mark, Don't wait up! I've decided to hit the town with Simon and Paul. I've nicked your Beetle crushers, am I forgiven?

FEELINGS through the tone of your writing.

SKILL - through your use of language.

LETTERS SHOW

YOURSELF either formally or informally they reveal something about you.

INFORMATION - through what you say.

Rules for Layout

N.B. These are adhered to closely for a formal letter and less so as you go down the scale of formality.

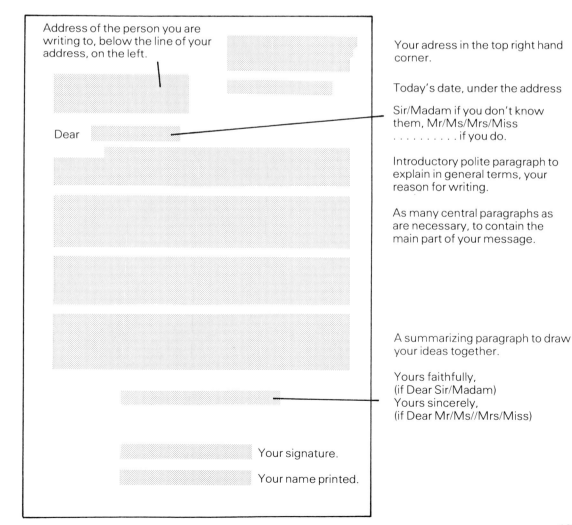

Address of the person you are writing to, below the line of your address, on the left.

Dear

Your adress in the top right hand corner.

Today's date, under the address

Sir/Madam if you don't know them, Mr/Ms/Mrs/Miss . . . . if you do.

Introductory polite paragraph to explain in general terms, your reason for writing.

As many central paragraphs as are necessary, to contain the main part of your message.

A summarizing paragraph to draw your ideas together.

Yours faithfully, (if Dear Sir/Madam) Yours sincerely, (if Dear Mr/Ms//Mrs/Miss)

Your signature.

Your name printed.

How would you set out the following? What tone would you adopt?

1 A letter to a travel agent, confirming the arrival of your tickets.
2 A letter to your mother or father asking for more student's grant.
3 A letter to ask for unemployment benefit.
4 A letter to tell your sister that you called round when she was out.
5 A letter to put in the milk bottle to ask for an extra pint.

Who is the sender and the recipient of the following letters?

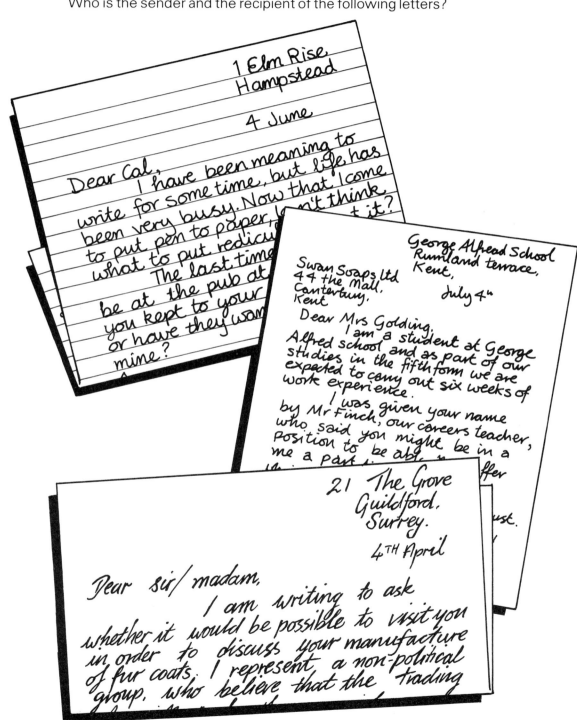

1 Elm Rise,
Hampstead

4 June

Dear Cal,
I have been meaning to write for some time, but life has been very busy. Now that I come to put pen to paper, don't think what to put. ridicu...t it?
The last time... be at the pub at... you kept to your... or have they wan... mine?

George Alfred School
Rumland terrace,
Kent,
July 4th

Swan Soaps Ltd
44 the Mall,
Canterbury,
Kent

Dear Mrs Golding,
I am a student at George Alfred school and as part of our studies in the fifth form we are expected to carry out six weeks of work experience.
I was given your name by Mr Finch, our careers teacher, who said you might be in a position to be abl... me a part... ...ffer ...ust.

21 The Grove
Guildford,
Surrey.

4TH April

Dear sir/madam,
I am writing to ask whether it would be possible to visit you in order to discuss your manufacture of fur coats. I represent a non-political group, who believe that the trading

Narrative Writing

When you write a story you have to decide where you are going to be in relation to it:

Outside the story –
a third person narrative.

Half inside the story –
semi-impersonal narrator.

Inside the story –
first person narrative.

Narrative writing involves a decision by a writer as to whether or not to come inside her/his story, either as a character of their invention, or perhaps as themselves.

In some stories the narrator is the main focus of the story, in others just a mouthpiece for the close description of another more interesting character or place. For this reason the narrator tends either to be the average person who observes well, or a person whose life has been extraordinary. Whichever it is, the aim of the narrator is to draw the reader in.

Description and dialogue

Even in a first person narrative, the story will usually include reported speech and description. In a third person narrative you are more likely to find actual dialogue (rather than reported speech), and a greater amount of description.

Timescale

Timescale is also important in narrative style. In most cases the narrator recalls something which happened to him/her several weeks, months or years before.

I have a great deal of difficulty in beginning to write my portion of these pages, for I know I am not clever. I always knew that. I can remember, when I was a very little girl indeed, I used to say to my doll, when we were alone together, 'Now, Dolly, I am not clever, you know very well, and you must be patient with me, like a dear!' And so she used to sit propped up in a great arm-chair, with her beautiful complexion and rosy lips, staring at me – or not so much at me, I think, as at nothing – while I busily stitched away, and told her every one of my secrets.

Often the story itself takes over, and the narrator slips into the background, so that the narrative appears to be happening in the present.

While we were in London, Mr Jarndyce was constantly beset by the crowd of excitable ladies and gentlemen whose proceedings had so much astonished us. Mr Quale, who presented himself soon after our arrival, was in all such excitements. He seemed to project those two shining knobs of temples of his into everything that went on, and to brush his hair farther and farther back, until the very roots were almost ready to fly out of his head in inappeasable philanthropy.

Charles Dickens

As you come to write a narrative you need to decide where you stand in time. This will determine whether you choose to use the present, past or future tense.

The past	The present	The future
Books about childhood/ teenage/young adult experiences.	Used in crime fiction where the private eye tells the case as it happens.	Used in science fiction.
past tense	*present tense*	*future tense*

Of course, some stories hop between different times. They often begin in the present and take you, in a flash-back fashion, to the past, before returning to the present again. The reordering of time proves an interesting addition to stories, as it avoids them being predictable chronological accounts.

Instructive and Report Writing

The purpose of instructive or report writing is to convey a clear message to someone else, or to record an event permanently.

Here are some examples:

Instructions
- a recipe
- a car repair manual
- life saving instructions
- the instructions of how to assemble a child's toy

Reports
- a school report
- an accident report
- an eye-witness account of a robbery
- the minutes of a meeting

In instructions and reports, the account is usually meant to be without the bias of personal opinion. They are supposed to contain only factual information, but in the case of report writing, bias can creep in, as people remember and interpret events in an individual way.

Instructive Writing

Instructions can be:

Verbal
- a recipe on the radio

Non-verbal
- a repair manual

They need to convey information clearly. Sometimes they assume a reader has a certain amount of knowledge (computer manuals) and at other times they assume she/he has none (Origami book).

They need to be:
- clear,
- concise,
- step by step.

See if you can write instructions like these for:

1 Completing a task in an English lesson.
2 Setting up a science experiment.
3 Making a bed.

Report writing

This is often a process of summarizing something you have seen or heard, into a quick, easy-to-read format.

Accident report

The old man crossed the road, thinking it was clear. A car pulled out from the righthand side, and sped over the crossing, knocking the old man over.

Discussion report

We discussed the statistics on the rise in popularity of the quiz show, and decided that the main reasons were its low budget, the chance for a poor person to become rich, the use of ordinary people, and the element of chance.

Below is an eye-witness account of a mugging, followed by a shortened report kept by the police.

> *'There was three of them, 'orrible they was, all powered up and thinking they was the bees knees. I think they'd been drinking too. Well, Mrs Norris, she's the lady they done in, she was just goin' along, mindin' her own business, when they come at her from behind. She was just by the chip shop by then. They hit her on the head, and when she turned round I saw her face was bleedin' somethin' wicked! Well the little bloke, he hit her again and she fell down. I think she scratched his face first though 'cause he was bleedin' too. The tall bloke took her bag, and the woman grabbed inside her coat, for money I suppose. Then they ran off down Archway, past the bingo place.'*

> *Thursday 8th March. 5.30pm.*
> *Two men and one woman attacked Mrs D. Norris, on Forwards Lane, outside the Sun King chip shop. Mrs Norris was struck once on the back of the head and once in the stomach. She had her bag and wallet stolen. The three youths made an escape down Kennel Rise, Archway.*

See if you can condense the following passage into a report format.

> *I saw the teenagers coming out of the disco at about 9.30. I know it was then because the news had just finished, and I'd gone to make some tea. I think the fight had already begun inside the hall, because they came out in a scuffle, and there were some cross words exchanged. But the first blow I saw was from a tall white boy, in a denim jacket. He seemed to be picking on a smaller boy with fair hair. Once he struck out, the three smaller boys, who looked like brothers just laid into the tall boy until he was on the ground and lifeless. I called the police then, but when I came back one of the three brothers was flat out on the ground too, so I don't know how that happened.*

Review Writing

What can you review?

Why review?

- to fix something in your reader's memory;
- to express a personal opinion about something;
- to assess something's value, in relation to other examples of the same (was it a 'good' play?);
- to pin-point aspects of particular interest;
- to show your own knowledge of what you review, or of the medium generally;
- to win over your reader, and persuade them to share the same experience (buy the book, go to see the film);
- to dissuade your reader from sharing the experience (a bad review).

The review on page 165 attempts to do several of these things. Pick out the words and phrases which meet each of the points above.

Now attempt to write your own review encompassing all of the checkpoints above. Make sure that it is something which is fresh in your mind.

Beginnings and endings

These are the most important part of reviews as they hold an impact for readers, and help them to make a decision about what is reviewed.

Below are some beginnings and endings. Which do you find the most interesting and effective and why?

'Watching a play by Osborne is like opening a door on yourself.'

'I wasn't sure if I was going to like a three hour long play by Shakespeare, but I actually enjoyed it and found it funny.'

'I'll leave you with one piece of the play which is a truly great speech. Jacques the speaker:

"All the worlds a stage, and all the men and women merely players." Shakespeare leaves us something from which we can remember him by.'

'The play ended. Actors off, curtain down, all those questions left unanswered.'

Persuading the reader

> You may find the Skills Section on persuasion in argumentative essays, on page 152, useful here.

Vocabulary and Context

Your choice of vocabulary says a great deal about your opinion of what you are reviewing.

Which of the following review statements are *positive* and which are *negative*?

- The soprano had a rather shrill voice.
- He moved delicately across the stage.
- The production was crisp and exciting.
- The scenery was sparse.
- The set had a dull effect.

To a large extent it depends upon the *context* of your writing. Sometimes reviewers speak sarcastically:

'He moved delicately across the stage.' This might be a compliment to a ballet dancer, but an insult to a miscast ogre!

Comparisons

These are useful in reviews, either to make a serious point or to undermine and ridicule.

'The production of Swan Lake was more like a dip in the bird bath than a graceful glide down the river. Part of this effect was created by the move away from traditional white costumes, and part of it by an over zealous flapping of arms from the prima ballerina.'

Word choice

Sometimes a precise choice of wording shows the writer's views. What is the difference in tone between the following words?

wet	dank
simple	simplistic
leaking	oozing
smell	stench
stare	leer
sharp	razor-like
untidy	sluttish

The words on the right are called 'emotive', because they don't just give information but they suggest how the reader should feel about the subject too.

REVIEW OF 'AS YOU LIKE IT'

William Shakespeare's comedy 'As You Like It' has no doubt been performed countless times, in many different places and in many different ways. Watching it at the Barbican Theatre was the first time I had seen a Shakespeare play at a theatre so it was completely new to me.

Before the play started the set consisted of an empty wooden stage with a blue circular area at the centre which seemed to be padded in some way. There was a plain white wall at the back of the stage into which what seemed to be a perfect half spherical alcove had been cut. A small flight of steps led from the stage to this alcove.

The stage arrangement looked so simple. I had expected something in the line of a painted background scene or a detailed set. This set was certainly original, but how would they use it?

As the first act progressed I began to realise, much to my surprise, that the Shakespearian words began to make sense and soon it became, as I got used to it, easy to understand. More so than if you just read the play straight off. I found myself enjoying the script and understanding some of the jokes. The whole spirit and flow of the play was kept very much alive by the actors who's performances were powerful, convincing and lively.

The actors fitted their parts perfectly: Orlando was young, energetic, defiant and determined. Rosalind had similar characteristics as well as being elegant. Celia, her cousin, was particularly good. She played a less pretty and energetic person with, at times, a rather rye sense of humour. Throughout the play she seemed to be the mature "big sister" to Rosalind. Touchstone the jester was witty and outspoken.

The mirror-reflective curtain lifted on the second half to reveal a stage now lit green with a large white sheet hanging from the ceiling which covered part of the stage. The sheet in turn lifted to reveal the same props as before but this time green in colour. This colour change was intending to give the feeling that the area was now in a forest in the countryside.

Rosalind, now disguised as a young man (not very convincingly), has bought up a farm which she, Celia and Touchstone are now living on. Orlando, who has met up with her father, the exiled Duke, is lovesick for the girl he has once met in the palace, this girl is of course Rosalind. Soon, he and the disguised Rosalind bump into each other. She knows it is Orlando, although he does not recognise her, and promises to cure his lovesickness by pretending to be Rosalind. Their brief meetings are overlooked by an embarassed Celia who usually skulks in the background, reading a book or doing yoga, she gives an excellent performance.

At the mass-wedding Rosalind reveals her true identity and as a result of a complicated bet Silvius and Phebe, along with Rosalind and Orlando, marry. During the festive wedding ceremony everyone is very happy, especially the exiled Duke who now has his daughter back. Songs are sung and Touchstone with his inimitable style acts out some of his wise

teachings with often outrageous movements.
On the whole 'As You Like It' was an enjoyable, well acted play which included some simple but brilliant special effects.

William Paylin.

Introduction

The GCSE places great importance on oral skills. But what are they?

Being skilled orally is not just a matter of being able to *talk* but it is also about being able to *listen*. The most skilled people, are those who can maintain a balance between speaking and listening.

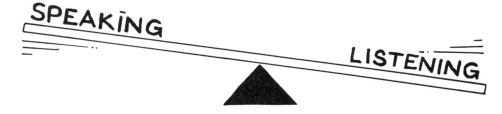

Oral work is also important for *thinking*. Sometimes it's difficult to be clear about an idea until you have listened to another's viewpoint, or simply verbalized it yourself.

In most English oral tasks, you need to think about your:

	Subject	Formality	Audience	End result
A	Nuclear weapons	a talk to the whole class	whole class	a clear commentary
B	School uniform	work in pairs	one other person	notes on the advantages and disadvantages of having a uniform

Your speaking and listening will need to be gauged according to each of these four areas.

Subject

A *Nuclear weapons*
Some complex, and previously unknown vocabulary will need to be explained i.e. deterrent, atomic.

B *School uniform*
Vocabulary is likely to be known by all i.e. blazer, rules, and need not therefore be explained.

Formality

A *To the whole class*
What you say has to be worked out in advance, in order to avoid hesitations and unclear meanings. You need to have notes to prompt your speech.

B *In a pair*
More natural speech can be used, which allows for hesitations, 'um's and 'er's. 'Discovery' language can also be used in which you test out expressions and ways of saying something, refining them in order to state your exact meaning.

Audience

The whole class
You need to be aware of how much the audience knows already, and angle your talk to their interests.

In a pair
Working with one other person allows you to rephrase your ideas if they aren't understood, and so build up a good relationship for discussion.

End result

All tasks have an end result. In your work within each task, you must bear this end result in mind. So, if the point of your task is to have clear notes, you need to steer your discussion to allow for this.

If your end result is to inform a whole class, then you need to ensure that they have taken in what you've said.

Specific Tasks

The four most commonly set tasks to test your oral abilities are:

- reading out a prepared passage;
- listening to a passage;
- role play;
- a prepared talk.

Below are some techniques which may prove useful, in preparing for these tasks.

Reading Out a Prepared Passage

Preparation is the keyword here. One simple way to prepare is to:

- read the passage through twice;
- write down the main points of the passage, to make sure you've understood it;
- devise a scheme for marking words, in pencil, in order to remind yourself when to pause, when to speak with extra emphasis, when to speak loudly or softly;
- practise reading with the annotation at normal speed (you can tape yourself and play it back, to see if you make the passage clear).

Below are two passages. The first is annotated for you. Read it through correctly and then go through the above procedure, in order to prepare the second passage.

Code: quieter   >
      louder   <
      short breath ⌐
      long breath ⌐
      pause for audience to laugh/react ℓ
      emphasize word _____

From *The Sniper* by Liam O'Flaherty

Cautiously he raised himself and peered over the parapet. ⌐ There was a flash and a bullet whizzed over his head. He dropped immediately. He had seen the flash. It came from the opposite side of the street. ⌐

He rolled over the roof to a chimney stack in the rear, and slowly drew himself up behind it, until his eyes were level with the top of the parapet. There was nothing to be seen – just the dim outline of the opposite housetop against the blue sky. His <u>enemy</u> was under cover. ℓ

Just then an armoured car came across the bridge and advanced slowly up the street. It stopped on the opposite side of the street fifty yards ahead. The sniper could hear the dull panting of the motor. ⌐ His heart beat faster. It was an <u>enemy</u> car. ⌐ He wanted to fire, but he knew it was useless. His bullets would never pierce the steel that covered the grey monster. ℓ

Then round the corner of a side street came an old woman, her head covered by a tattered shawl. She began to talk to the man in the turret of the car. She was pointing to the roof where the sniper lay. An <u>informer</u>.

The turret opened. The man's head and shoulders appeared, looking towards the sniper. The sniper raised his rifle and fired. ⌐ The head fell heavily on the turret wall. The woman darted toward the side street. The sniper fired again. The woman whirled around and fell with a <u>shriek</u> into the gutter. ℓ

Suddenly from the opposite roof a shot rang out and the sniper dropped his rifle with a curse. The rifle clattered to the roof. The sniper thought the noise would wake the dead. He stopped to pick the rifle up. He couldn't lift it. His foream was dead. '<u>Christ</u>,' he muttered, 'I'm <u>hit</u>.'

171

Dropping flat on the roof he crawled back to the parapet. With his left hand he felt the injured right forearm. The blood was oozing through the sleeve of his coat. There was no pain – just a deadened sensation, as if the arm had been cut off. ⌐

Quickly he drew his knife from his pocket, opened it on the breastwork of the parapet, and ripped open the sleeve. There was a small hole where the bullet had entered. On the other side there was no hole. The bullet had lodged in the bone. It must have fractured it. He bent the arm below the wound. The arm bent back easily. He ground his teeth to overcome the pain. ⌐

Then, taking out his field dressing, he ripped open the packet with his knife. H broke the neck of the iodine bottle and let the bitter fluid drip into the wound. A paroxysm of pain swept through him He placed the cotton wadding over the wound and wrapped the dressing over i He tied the end with his teeth. ⌐

Then he lay still against the parapet, and closing his eyes he made an effort t overcome the pain.

In the street beneath all was still. ⌐ T armoured car had retired speedily over the bridge, with the machine gunner's head hanging lifeless over the turret. The woman's corpse lay still in the gutter.

The Sniper: main points

- gunman narrator on a roof;
- someone fires at him;
- enemy armoured car comes up the street;
- narrator sees a woman informing the armoured car of his presence;
- the gunman is shot by someone from the opposite roof.

From *Gawain and the Lady Ragnell* by Ethel Johnston Phelps

Long ago, in the days of King Arthur, the finest knight in all Britain was the king's nephew Gawain. He was, by reputation, the bravest in battle, the wisest, the most courteous, the most compassionate, and the most loyal to his king.

One day in late summer, Gawain was with Arthur and the knights of the court at Carlisle in the north. The king returned from the day's hunting looking so pale and shaken that Gawain followed him at once to his chamber.

"What has happened, my Lord?" asked Gawain with concern.

Arthur sat down heavily. "I had a very strange encounter in the Inglewood forest . . . I hardly know what to make of

it." And he related to Gawain what had occurred.

"Today I hunted a great white stag," sa Arthur. "The stag at last escaped me an I was alone, some distance from my me Suddenly a tall, powerful man appeare before me with a sword upraised."

"And you were unarmed!"

"Yes. I had only one bow and a dagger i my belt. He threatened to kill me," Arthur went on. "And he swung his sword as though he meant to cut me down on the spot! Then he laughed horribly and said he would give me one chance to save my life."

"Who was this man?" cried Gawain. "Why should he want to kill you?"

"He said his name was Sir Gromer, and he sought revenge for the loss of his northern lands."

"A chieftain from the north!" exclaimed Gawain. "But what is the one chance he spoke of?"

"I gave him my word I would meet him one year from today, unarmed, at the same spot, with the answer to a question!" said Arthur.

Gawain started to laugh, but stopped at once when he saw Arthur's face. "A question! Is it a riddle? And one year to find the answer? That should not be hard!"

Listening to a Passage

You usually listen to a passage in order to take it in, remember it, understand it and comment upon it. Many things are necessary to make this kind of listening possible.

Mental attitude

If your brain is clouded with thoughts, then your mind will drift while the person is reading. Before the person begins to read, you need to concentrate your mind on what you are about to hear.

Physical attitude

'Are you sitting comfortably? Then I'll begin.' used to be the first words of a radio story reading. Being restless and uncomfortable will prevent you from concentrating (as well as distracting others). You need to be completely silent, not just not speaking, but not rustling plastic bags, or flicking pens either! A reader will want to build upon silences in their reading, not classroom noises!

Remember keywords

You will not remember a whole passage, but you need to remember some of its main ideas. One useful approach is to remember keywords. The first sentence of a passage is often important, as it establishes the time scale, setting and subject of the passage. Here is a passage where the keywords have been highlighted.

Heat the colour of fire, sky as heavy as mud, and under both the soil – hard, dry, unyielding.

It was a silent harvest. Across the valley, the yellow rice fields stretched, stooped and dry. The sun glazed the afternoon with a heat so fierce that the distant mountains shimmered in it. The dust in the sky, the cracked earth, the shrivelled leaves fluttering on brittle branches – everything was scorched.

Fanning out in a jagged line across the fields were the harvesters, their sickles flashing in the sun. Nobody spoke. Nobody laughed. Nobody sang. The only noise was wave after wave of sullen hisses as the rice stalks were slashed and flung to the ground.

A single lark flew by, casting a swift shadow on the stubbled fields. From under the brim of her hat, Jinda saw it wing its way west. It flew to a tamarind tree at the foot of the mountain, circled it three times and flew away.

A good sign, Jinda thought. Maybe the harvest won't be so poor after all. She straightened up her spine, and gazed at the brown fields before her. In all her seventeen years, Jinda had never seen a crop as bad as this one. The heads of grain were so light the rice stalks were hardly bent under their weight. Jinda peeled at the husk of one grain: the rice grain inside was no thicker than a fingernail.

Here is a checklist to test how well you assimilated the information in the passage.

- Describe the setting.
- Is it present day/past/future?
- Who is in the passage?
- What is taking place?

Role Play

In most cases, your teacher will give you clear guidelines for role play, which will alter depending on the task. Here are some general points to remember.

'Throw yourself into' any character you are intended to speak for. The more you try to identify with the character, the more you will gain from the exercise. Having been told who you are, you need to form a total person around the idea. Think about:

- your tone of voice;
- the pitch, or sound of your voice;
- your non-verbal communication;
- your habit-formed actions;
- your chosen attitude to the given issue.

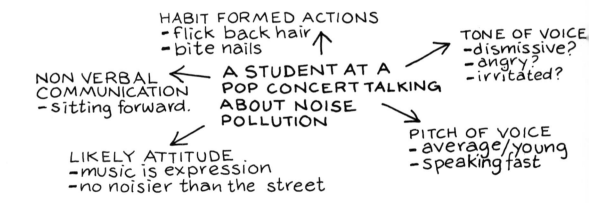

Try to build up a picture of the whole person in each of the following cases.

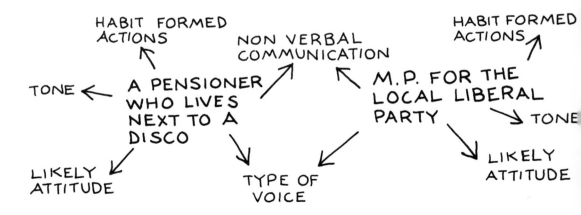

Avoid reproducing stereotyped characters. Try to really get inside the other person's skin, so as to put their point of view more forcibly.

Listen to the other people involved in the role play, and respond to their ideas. Don't pre-plan everything you intend to say, allow your self to adlib and be adaptable.

Don't be thrown by people not behaving as you expect. React to them as they *are*, not as you *think* they should be.

Draw on all your experience of real people, to create your imaginary person. Make your characters believable.

A Prepared Talk

> The *note-taking* section, on page 146, within this Skills Section, will give you some ideas of how to prepare for the talk, and building up useful notes.

A prepared talk is one of the most difficult oral tasks, and the one where your audience is perhaps the most important factor. You need to keep your audience interested, and ensure that they understand you fully. Here are some pointers to help:

1 Speak clearly and confidently. Avoid fidgeting, or making actions which distract from your words.
2 Have clear notes for your talk, but don't write out what you intend to say word for word.
3 Base your ideas around main points that are easy to remember, perhaps having all key words beginning with the same letter:

Industrialization –   **M**anufacturing in factories
                         Marketing goods – selling
                         Moving to towns to find work
                         Machine work – in factories

4 Provide visual images in what you *say* so that the listener remembers them in her/his mind.

   'One aspect of a child's development is like that of a chick. The egg hatches but this is not the end of the growing process, the young chick is still vulnerable to many dangers. Likewise the child's birth is by no means the end of its dependence on the mother.'
5 Use visual aids; pictures, artefacts, slides or video, to punctuate your talk with interesting stimuli. People remember what they *see*, far better than what they *hear*. Even if you simply wrote up your main points as keywords on the blackboard, this would help.
6 Incorporate more than one voice in the talk. Either co-opt another class member to read out extracts from magazines, or papers, or give the opinion of an individual. If you can't co-opt for this exercise, then allow yourself to speak with a different tone, or at a different pitch, when representing different people.
7 Regulate your own speaking voice. No one wants to listen to a dull monotone! Make your voice interesting, by allowing it to vary its pace, pitch and tone.
8 Involve your audience in what you say:
   - keep checking that they have understood;
   - ask their opinions;
   - get them to point out things you have previously highlighted, to check that they have followed your talk;
   - give them time for questions.

Acknowledgements

The Publishers' thanks are due to the following for permission to reproduce copyright material:

page 6: William Heinemann Ltd for lines taken from 'When You're a Jet' from the musical *West Side Story* by Leonard Bernstein and Stephen Sondhe
page 7: William Samson for 'One of the Boys'; *page 10:* Faber and Faber Ltd for 'Rondeau Redouble' by Wendy Cope from *Making Cocoa for Kingsley A*
by Wendy Cope; *page 11:* The Women's Press for 'I'm Really Very Fond' from *Horses Make a Landscape Look More Beautiful* by Alice Walker; *page*
Faber and Faber Ltd for the extract from *Look Back in Anger* by John Osborne; *page 14 and 15:* Graham Agency, New York, for the extracts from
Golden Pond by Ernest Thompson; *page 17:* Ann Hunter for 'Love Poem' from *No Holds Barred* published by The Women's Press; *page 18:* Holly Bee
for 'The Children Sleep Soundly Upstairs' from *No Holds Barred* published by The Women's Press; *page 19:* ILEA English Centre for the extract f
'Jamaica Child' by Erol O'Connor from *Our Lives; page 20:* Michael Joseph Ltd for the extract from *A Fortunate Grandchild* by Miss Read; *page 22:* Un
Hyman Ltd for 'A Blade of Grass' by Brian Patten from *Love Poems*; Hodder and Stoughton for 'Declaration of Intent' by Steve Turner from *Up to D*
Sara O'Reilly for 'Together We are Building a Wall' from *Bonds* edited by Pat D'Arcy; *page 23:* Bloodaxe Books for 'A Death in Winter' by Jeni Cou
from *Life By Drowning* (1983); *The Mail on Sunday (You* magazine) for the article on baby Nicola Bell; *page 25:* Curtis Brown Ltd for the extract fr
'The Valentine Generation' by John Wain from *The Valentine Generation and other Stories* (1980) published by Longman; *page 30:* Martin Secke
Warburg for the extract from 'Why I Write' by George Orwell from *Collected Essays, Journalism and Letters of George Orwell Volume 1; page 31:* La
Cecil for 'Personal Essay' by Adèle Geras first published by Bell & Hyman Ltd in *Stepping Out* edited by Jane Leggett, © 1987 Adèle Geras; *page*
The Daily Telegraph for the mini sagas 'What the Sleeping Beauty Would Have Given Her Right Arm For' by Zoe Ellis and 'Homecoming' by Roger Wo
from *The Book of Mini Sagas; page 34 and 35:* Vallentine Mitchell & Co Ltd for two extracts from Anne Frank's Diary; *page 36:* Associated B
Publishers (UK) Ltd for the extract from *Go Ask Alice* anon; *page 37:* Aitken & Stone Ltd for the extract from *Catcher in the Rye* by J.D. Salinger publis
by Hamish Hamilton; Associated Book Publishers (UK) Ltd for the extract from *The Secret Diary of Adrian Mole 13¾* by Sue Townsend; *page 38:* Mich
Joseph Ltd for the extract from 'The Desperadoes' by Stan Barstow from *The Desperadoes; page 40:* The Women's Press for the extract from '1955' fr
It's Now or Never by Alice Walker; *page 41:* The Women's Press for the extract from 'Elethia' from *You Can't Keep a Good Woman Down* by Alice Wal
page 45: Michael Joseph Ltd for the extract from 'The Human Element' by Stan Barstow from *The Desperadoes; page 46:* Warner Bros Music Lim
for the song script 'Masters of War' by Bob Dylan © M Witmark & Sons 1963; *page 47:* A & M Records Ltd for the song script 'Russians' by Sting; *p*
48: The Observer for the article 'Women at the Wire' by Hugo Davenport, December 1982; *page 54:* Only Women Press for 'The Birth' by Jennifer Gu
page 57: ILEA English Centre for 'The Abuse of Animals' by Tanya Nyari in *Say What You Think; page 59:* Chatto & Windus for the extract from *S*
of Solomon by Toni Morrison; *page 61 and 132:* Action Aid for the publicity leaflet 'Poverty Fighter'; *page 62:* World Vision for the publicity leaflet 'Wh
Life is Cheap a Child's Life is Cheapest'; *page 64:* Virago Press for 'Still I Rise' by Maya Angelou; *page 67:* Times Newspapers Ltd for the extract fr
'A Life in the Day of Diane Harpwood' taken from *The Sunday Times Magazine; page 69: Today,* Times Newspapers Ltd and *The Independent* for
front pages of their newspapers for Monday 23 February 1987; *page 70:* Hodder and Stoughton Ltd for 'Exclusive Pictures' by Steve Turner from *U*
Date; page 71: The Observer for the article 'The Seige' by Le Carré; *page 73: The Observer* for the article 'News at Ten'; *page 75 and 76:* Syndicat
International for 'Cry Baby' which appeared in *Photolove* published by IPC Magazines; D C Comics Inc for pages from *Tales of the Teen Titans No*
© 1987 Hasbro Inc for 'The Greatest Gift' from *Jem; page 78:* Faber and Faber Ltd for 'Advertisement' from *Making Cocoa for Kingsley Amis* by Wer
Cope; Tobyward Limited for the advertisement 'Dumpy to Dazzling'; *page 79:* Hodder and Stoughton Ltd for 'Tonight We Will Fake Love' by Steve Tur
from *Up to Date;* Venus Beauty Products for the advertisement 'Solve Your Skin Problem'; *page 80 and 81: The Independent, The Daily Telegraph*
The Guardian for the Action Directe articles; *page 82:* Cosmopolitan for the article 'Could You Pass the Teacher Test' by Gillian Capper; *page 84:* Vira
and Quartet Books for the extract from *Forgetting is no Excuse* by Mary Stott; *page 85:* Pluto Press for 'Maintenance Engineer' by Sandra Kay; *page*
Daphne Schiller for 'I Had Rather be a Woman' from *No Holds Barred* published by The Women's Press Ltd, 1985; Anna Swir for 'The Washerwom
from *I'm the Woman; page 87:* Oxford University Press for the extract from *Brother in the Land* by Robert Swindells (1984); *page 89:* SCDC Publicatio
for the 'What £1 bought in 1914, 1934 and 1954' articles; *page 91: The Observer* for the article 'Chasing the Dragon' by Tony Moss; *page 92:* DHSS
the advertisement 'Hair Care by Heroin'; *page 93:* Hodder and Stoughton for 'Conquerors' by Henry Treece from *World of Challenge* by Sweeney; *p*
95: George Sassoon for 'The Child at the Window' by Siegfried Sassoon; *page 98:* Abner Stein for the extract from 'The Pedestrian' by Ray Bradbu
page 101: Victor Gollancz Ltd for the extract from *I Am the Cheese* by Robert Cormier; *page 103:* Pan Books for the extract from *Hitch-Hiker's Gu*
to the Galaxy by Douglas Adams; *page 106 and 107:* Hodder and Stoughton Ltd for the extract from *The Thousand Eyes of Night* by Robert Swinde
page 108 and 133: 'Late Home' © Trevor Millum, reprinted by permission of the author; *page 113:* Macdonald for 'Humanoids . . . and Strange Insign
from the series *The Unexplained; page 116:* Sidgwick and Jackson for the extract from *Is That It?* by Bob Geldof; *page 118:* Times Newspapers Ltd
the extract from *Pauline Peters on People: The Lonely Ladies of Manhattan* © Times Newspapers Ltd 1988; *page 120:* Centreprise Publications for
extract 'George Wood Mortuary Technician' from *Working Lives Volume 2 Hackney 1945–1977; page 121:* © Jenny Joseph from *Beyond Descar*
published by Secker and Warburg 1983; *page 122:* The estate of F. Scott Fitzgerald for the extract from *The Great Gatsby* by F. Scott Fitzgerald publish
by The Bodley Head; *page 123 and 133:* Anthony Sheil Associates for the extract from *The French Lieutenant's Woman* by John Fowles; *page 125:* Fa
and Faber Ltd for the extract from *Squaring the Circle* by Tom Stoppard; *page 127:* William Collins Sons & Co Ltd for the extract from *It's My Life*
Robert Leeson © 1980; *page 129:* Heinemann Educational Books for the extract from *A Man for all Seasons* by Robert Bolt; *page 133 and 145:* An
Deutsch for the letters from *84 Charing Cross Road* by Helene Hanff; *page 134:* copyright © 1959 by Alan Sillitoe from *The Long Distance Runn*
reprinted by permission of Tessa Sayle Agency; Chatto and Windus for the extract from *The L-Shaped Room* by Lynn Reed Banks; *page 136:* Adèle Ger
for the article 'Greensleeves' which appeared in the *New Statesman* 19 July 1987; *page 143:* Camden New Journal for the article 'Celebrities say: han
off library'; *page 144:* J M Dent and Sons for the extract from *In the Shadow of the Wind* by Anne Herbert; *page 154:* permission granted by Curtis Bro
Ltd on behalf of Daphne du Maurier for the extract from *Rebecca* copyright © 1983 by Daphne du Maurier Browning; Antonia Barber for the extr
from *The Amazing Mr Blunden; page 155:* Faber and Faber Ltd for 'Nights in the Iron Hotel' by Michael Hoffman from *Nights in the Iron Hotel; pa*
171: Jonathan Cape Ltd for the extract from 'The Sniper' by Liam O'Flaherty from *The Short Stories of Liam O'Flaherty; page 172:* Henry Holt and
Inc for the extract from 'Gawain and the Lady Ragnell' from *The Maid of the North* by Ethel Johnston Phelps.

The Publishers have made every effort to clear copyrights and trust that their apologies will be accepted for any errors or omissions. They will be pleas
to hear from any copyright holder who has not received due acknowledgement, though where no reply was received to their letters requesting permissi
the Publishers have assumed that there was no objection to their using the material.

The Publishers would also like to thank the following pupils of William Ellis School, London for permission to use their work:

Tom Bilton for 'Mirror Eyes at the Doctors'; Nathan Williams for 'The Final Punishment'; Jason Caffrey for 'Alice in Wonderland'; Darius Bazergen
'Unsung Heroes Called Fanatics' and 'Italian Beauty'; William Paylin for the review of 'As You Like It'.